LAWS AND PROGRAMS

TRUSTED TRAVELER PROGRAMS

TRENDS AND IMPACTS

LAWS AND PROGRAMS

Additional books in this series can be found on Nova's website under the Series tab.

Additional e-books in this series can be found on Nova's website under the e-book tab.

LAWS AND PROGRAMS

TRUSTED TRAVELER PROGRAMS

TRENDS AND IMPACTS

BLAIRE FORESTER
EDITOR

New York

For permission to use material from this book please contact us:
Telephone 631-231-7269; Fax 631-231-8175
Web Site: http://www.novapublishers.com

Additional color graphics may be available in the e-book version of this book.

Library of Congress Cataloging-in-Publication Data

ISBN: 978-1-63321-830-7

Published by Nova Science Publishers, Inc. † New York

CONTENTS

PREFACE

Chapter 1 – Nearly 1 million people and $1.5 billion of trade entered the United States through 328 POEs on an average day in fiscal year 2013. CBP, within the Department of Homeland Security (DHS), has four trusted traveler programs—Global Entry, NEXUS, SENTRI, and Free and Secure Trade (FAST)—to provide for expedited travel through dedicated lanes and kiosks at POEs. GAO was asked to review these programs. This report addresses (1) trends in enrollment and program use over the past 5 fiscal years, (2) the extent to which CBP has designed and implemented processes to help ensure consistent and efficient enrollment of applicants, and (3) the impacts of the programs on travelers and CBP. GAO analyzed data on enrollment and POE operations from fiscal years 2009 through 2013, reviewed documents, and visited nine POEs selected based on traveler volume and location. While information from these POEs cannot be generalized, the visits provided insights on program operations.

Chapter 2 – This is a Statement of Colleen Manaher, Executive Director, Planning, Program Analysis, and Evaluation, U.S. Customs and Border Protection.

In: Trusted Traveler Programs
Editor: Blaire Forester

ISBN: 978-1-63321-830-7

Chapter 1

TRUSTED TRAVELERS: PROGRAMS PROVIDE BENEFITS, BUT ENROLLMENT PROCESSES COULD BE STRENGTHENED*

United States Government Accountability Office

WHY GAO DID THIS STUDY

Nearly 1 million people and $1.5 billion of trade entered the United States through 328 POEs on an average day in fiscal year 2013. CBP, within the Department of Homeland Security (DHS), has four trusted traveler programs—Global Entry, NEXUS, SENTRI, and Free and Secure Trade (FAST)—to provide for expedited travel through dedicated lanes and kiosks at POEs. GAO was asked to review these programs. This report addresses (1) trends in enrollment and program use over the past 5 fiscal years, (2) the extent to which CBP has designed and implemented processes to help ensure consistent and efficient enrollment of applicants, and (3) the impacts of the programs on travelers and CBP. GAO analyzed data on enrollment and POE operations from fiscal years 2009 through 2013, reviewed documents, and visited nine POEs selected based on traveler volume and location. While information from these POEs cannot be generalized, the visits provided insights on program operations.

---

* This is an edited, reformatted and augmented version of the United States Government Accountability Office publication, GAO-14-483, dated May 2014.

What GAO Recommends

GAO recommends, among other things, that CBP assess the feasibility of practices to improve application processing times, establish a mechanism to document types of interview questions asked, and document information on foreign countries' procedures. DHS concurred with all recommendations but one to establish a mechanism to document interview questions asked because, among other reasons, DHS does not believe it should use scripted interview questions. As discussed in this report, GAO continues to believe in the need for such a mechanism.

What GAO Found

As of January 2014, there were about 2.5 million people enrolled in U.S. Customs and Border Protection's (CBP) four trusted traveler programs—which provide expedited travel for preapproved, low-risk travelers and cargo—and enrollments more than quadrupled over the past 5 fiscal years. About 43 percent of trusted travelers were enrolled in Global Entry, operating at select air ports of entry (POE) and about 38 percent were enrolled in NEXUS, operating at northern border POEs. Trusted traveler entries into the United States increased from fiscal years 2009 through 2013. For example, entries through lanes for the Secure Electronic Network for Travelers Rapid Inspection (SENTRI) program, operating at southern border POEs, increased from 5.9 million to 12.6 million vehicles.

CBP has designed and implemented trusted traveler enrollment processes, but could improve key areas to enhance and assess consistency and efficiency in those processes. U.S. citizens and foreign nationals seek to enroll in CBP's trusted traveler programs through an application vetted by CBP and an in-person interview. CBP has taken steps to improve the efficiency of the application- vetting process by, for example, automating background checks. However, CBP has not assessed the feasibility of various other practices for improving efficiency in enrollment processes, such as conducting group briefings for applicants on the programs. As of August 2013, CBP had a backlog of pending applications, as there were about 90,000 applications pending CBP vetting, and another 33,000 applicants who had not scheduled an interview. Assessing the feasibility of various practices, consistent with program management standards, could better position CBP to improve application-processing times. Further, CBP has designed some processes for the trusted traveler applicant interview process to help ensure consistency across enrollment centers; however, GAO identified variations in interviews and application denial rates, indicating that interviews may not be conducted consistently across enrollment centers. For example, GAO observed interviews that did not consistently follow procedures laid out in CBP guidance at 2 of the 3 centers where GAO observed interviews. Establishing a mechanism for CBP officers to document the kinds of questions asked and the nature of the applicants' responses could better position CBP to help ensure that interviews are conducted consistently. In addition, CBP has implemented trusted traveler programs that allow participating low-risk citizens from nine countries to use Global Entry kiosks at select air POEs. CBP has discussed information about other countries' operational procedures for sharing applicant-vetting results, but has not documented this information for seven of the countries, consistent with internal control standards. Without such documentation, there is no institutional record that those countries' procedures for vetting applicants help to ensure that only low-risk applicants are enrolled.

Trusted travelers generally experience shorter wait times than regular travelers, and CBP spends less time inspecting trusted travelers at POEs than regular travelers. GAO's analysis of CBP data showed that primary inspections took about twice as long or longer on average for regular travelers than for trusted travelers at 11 of 14 SENTRI crossings and 12 of 18 NEXUS crossings in fiscal year 2013. GAO's analysis of CBP data also indicates that trusted travelers commit fewer border violations, such as smuggling, than regular travelers.

ABBREVIATIONS

CBP	U.S. Customs and Border Protection
CBSA	Canadian Border Services Agency
C-TPAT	Customs-Trade Partnership Against Terrorism
DHS	Department of Homeland Security
FAST	Free and Secure Trade
GES	Global Enrollment System
GOES	Global Online Enrollment System
OFO	Office of Field Operations
POE	port of entry

SENTRI	Secure Electronic Network for Travelers Rapid Inspection
TSA	Transportation Security Administration
WHTI	Western Hemisphere Travel Initiative

***

May 30, 2014

Congressional Requesters

On a typical day in fiscal year 2013, nearly 1 million passengers and pedestrians and over 67,000 truck, rail, and sea containers worth approximately $1.5 billion entered the United States through 328 U.S. land, sea, and air ports of entry (POE), according to U.S. Customs and Border Protection (CBP).[1] Within the Department of Homeland Security (DHS), CBP is the lead federal agency charged with a dual mission of keeping terrorists and their weapons, criminals and their contraband, and inadmissible aliens out of the country while also facilitating the flow of legitimate travel and trade at the nation's borders. CBP's Office of Field Operations (OFO) is responsible for cargo- and passenger-processing activities related to security, trade, immigration, and agricultural inspection at POEs.

CBP's focus has historically been on security; however, CBP has undertaken specific efforts to facilitate legitimate travel and trade. A key part of these efforts is CBP's development of four trusted traveler programs to expedite the travel of low-risk passengers and screened shipments across the border. More specifically, trusted traveler programs provide for expedited travel for preapproved, low-risk travelers—including U.S. citizens and foreign nationals—and cargo through dedicated lanes and kiosks at POEs. Individuals can apply for membership in all four of the trusted traveler programs online and, if conditionally approved, schedule an appointment with a CBP officer to undergo an enrollment interview, where applicants can be approved or denied membership in the programs. The four CBP trusted traveler programs are Secure Electronic Network for Travelers Rapid Inspection (SENTRI), NEXUS, Global Entry, and Free and Secure Trade (FAST). SENTRI offers expedited processing to approved low-risk travelers at southern land borders, while NEXUS primarily offers expedited processing to approved, low-risk travelers at the northern land border. Global Entry offers low-risk aviation passengers expedited processing at select aviation POEs. FAST allows low-risk commercial truckers expedited access at select commercial POEs at the northern (FAST North) and southern (FAST South) land borders.

You asked us to review CBP's trusted traveler programs to determine the extent to which the programs have improved the facilitation of legitimate travel and trade, including the efficiency of the application processes and the potential impacts on security. This report addresses the following questions:

1. What are the trends in enrollment and use of the trusted traveler programs over the past 5 fiscal years?
2. To what extent has CBP designed and implemented processes to help ensure the consistent and efficient enrollment of applicants in the trusted traveler programs?
3. What do data collected at POEs indicate about the impacts of the trusted traveler programs for travelers and CBP?

To inform our analysis of all three objectives, we visited nine POEs, including airports and land POEs, along or near the northern and southern borders. We selected the POEs in these locations on the basis of the locations having (1) higher than average traffic and participation in trusted traveler programs, (2) multiple POEs in geographic proximity to one another that participate in two or more trusted traveler programs, (3) enrollment centers—where applicants undergo an interview process when applying to be a trusted traveler—that collectively cover all four trusted traveler programs (SENTRI, NEXUS, Global Entry, and FAST), and (4) geographic dispersion to cover the southern and northern borders. The POEs we visited were Los Angeles International Airport; San Ysidro, California; Otay Mesa, California; Seattle-Tacoma International Airport; Blaine, Washington; Detroit Metropolitan Airport; Detroit, Michigan; and San Antonio International Airport and Laredo, Texas. While information we obtained from these visits cannot be generalized to all POEs, the visits provided us with insights into the operation of the trusted traveler programs.

To determine the trends in the enrollment and use of the trusted traveler programs over the past 5 fiscal years, we analyzed enrollment data from fiscal years 2009 through 2013 and selected membership and enrollment data as of January 2014. We met with CBP officials responsible for managing the enrollment system data to discuss data reliability, reviewed system documentation, and electronically tested the data. We determined that the data were sufficiently reliable for the purposes of this report. We also met with officials responsible for overseeing or conducting the enrollment interviews at all 12 enrollment centers at the locations we visited to gain a better understanding of the applicant interview process. We reviewed CBP data related to the numbers of trusted and regular travelers crossing the northern and southern land border crossings with dedicated trusted traveler lanes and through airports with Global Entry kiosks for fiscal years 2009 through 2013. To assess the reliability of these data, we reviewed documentation about CBP's data systems; interviewed agency officials responsible for managing, assessing, and using the data and the relevant systems; and electronically tested the data. We determined that the data were sufficiently reliable for the purposes of this report.

To determine the extent to which CBP has designed and implemented processes to help ensure the consistent and efficient enrollment of applicants in the trusted traveler programs, we reviewed the policies, procedures, and guidelines governing the trusted traveler enrollment process, such as the *Trusted Traveler Handbook*, policy memorandums, and bilateral arrangements with other countries.[2] To determine the extent to which the enrollment process resulted in consistent outcomes, we analyzed enrollment data from fiscal years 2009 through 2013 described above. When possible, we observed enrollment interviews and examined any locally developed guidance for conducting the enrollment interviews. We also reviewed and analyzed selected daily reports summarizing interview appointment availability from fiscal years 2013 and 2014. Additionally, we met with officials at CBP's Vetting Center and Ombudsman's office who manage the processes of vetting trusted traveler applications and reviewing cases where a person believes that his or her denial or revocation for participation in a program should be reconsidered. Further, we met with officials from CBP to discuss the procedures for developing bilateral arrangements and implementing joint trusted traveler programs with other countries. We observed enrollment center operations, interviewed CBP officials, and reviewed CBP documentation to assess the extent to which these enrollment processes were consistent with CBP guidelines, *Standards for Internal Control in the Federal Government,* Office of Management and Budget guidance on performance measures, and program management standards.[3] We also interviewed representatives from three associations, which we selected based on their representation of members of the travel or trade industries, to obtain their perspectives on the trusted traveler enrollment process. The perspectives of these associations are not generalizable to all of the travel and trade industries, but provided insights on the enrollment process and impacts of the trusted traveler programs.

To determine what data collected at POEs indicate about the impacts of the trusted traveler programs on travelers and CBP, we reviewed CBP data for fiscal years 2009 through 2013 related to the use of trusted traveler programs at POEs. These data include (1) the numbers and types of violations committed by trusted and regular travelers and (2) the differences in wait times and inspection times for trusted and regular travelers at crossings with trusted traveler lanes and kiosks. We reviewed CBP policies and guidance, such as the *Trusted Traveler Handbook*, memos describing accepted methodologies for calculating wait times, and CBP self-inspection reports. We interviewed CBP field officials at the nine POEs we visited about the operational impacts of the program related to security, traveler wait times, and the time it takes CBP to inspect travelers, and observed these impacts, including differences in infrastructure across POEs. We also interviewed CBP headquarters officials about the reliability of trusted and regular traveler wait time data, steps CBP is taking to improve the reliability of these data, and the extent to which CBP measures the impacts of the programs. In addition, we reviewed documentation and electronically tested the data in order to assess their reliability. We determined that the data were sufficiently reliable for the purposes of our report. However, we limited the scope of our work on wait times data, as CBP is currently taking steps to improve the reliability of the data. Data reliability considerations are discussed later in this report.

We conducted this performance audit from February 2013 to May 2014 in accordance with generally accepted government auditing standards. Those standards require that we plan and perform the audit to obtain sufficient, appropriate evidence to provide a reasonable basis for our findings and conclusions based on our audit objectives. We believe that the evidence obtained provides a reasonable basis for our findings and conclusions based on our audit objectives.

BACKGROUND

CBP's Four Trusted Traveler Programs

CBP's four trusted traveler programs are designed to allow for expedited travel for preapproved, low-risk travelers and cargo through dedicated lanes and kiosks at select POEs throughout the nation. The four trusted traveler programs are predicated on the vetting of travelers who have voluntarily applied for membership, paid a fee, and provided personal data to CBP.

Travelers who are granted trusted traveler status are considered lower risk than other travelers because of the vetting CBP conducts both when the travelers apply for program participation and after they become members. The programs, according to CBP officials, are part of the agency's risk-based security approach to focus resources, such as CBP officers, at the POEs on passengers and cargo that have not been identified as low risk. Table 1 provides information on each of CBP's trusted traveler programs.

Table 1. U.S. Customs and Border Protection (CBP) Trusted Traveler Programs

Trusted traveler program	Port of entry (POE) locations	Primary port of entry environment	Year begun	Eligible countries and citizenship
Secure Electronic Network for Travelers Rapid Inspection (SENTRI)	10 southern border POEs	Land	1995	Any
NEXUS	12 northern border POEs	Land, air, and sea	2002	Citizens or legal permanent residents of the United States or Canada
Free and Secure Trade (FAST)	8 southern and 4 northern border POEs	Commercial trucking	2002	Citizens or legal permanent residents of the United States, Canada, or Mexico
Global Entry	31 airports in the United States with incoming international flights and 10 airports in Canada and Ireland that clear passengers on outbound flights for entry into the United States	Air	2012[a]	Citizens or legal permanent residents of the United States, citizens of Germany, Mexico, the Netherlands, Qatar, the Republic of Korea, Panama, or the United Kingdom[b]

Source: GAO analysis of CBP data.

[a] Global Entry began as a pilot program in 2008 and became a permanent program in March 2012.

[b] Citizens from these countries are eligible to participate in Global Entry. As of March 2014, CBP considers arrangements with four of the seven countries to be in the pilot phase (Germany, Qatar, Panama, and the United Kingdom). In addition, CBP has completed bilateral arrangements with Israel and Saudi Arabia for participation in Global Entry; however, these pilots have not begun or have begun on a limited basis. According to CBP officials, CBP plans to expand the pilot with Saudi Arabia in the future. CBP has signed bilateral arrangements with Australia and New Zealand, but according to CBP officials, these countries have not established programs to allow their citizens to participate in Global Entry.

Processes for Enrolling in the Trusted Traveler Programs

To enroll in a trusted traveler program, applicants from the United States and other eligible countries must submit an initial application, pay a fee, have their information vetted by CBP, and undergo an in-person interview. Applicants apply for each of the four trusted traveler programs through CBP's Global Online Enrollment System (GOES). When applying, individuals submit information in GOES, including their name, address, date of birth, country of citizenship, and other pertinent information, such as which trusted traveler program they are applying for and payment information. Applicants also must answer questions included in the application on such topics as travel history, place of birth, and employment, among others. In addition, applicants must submit a nonrefundable payment for the processing of their applications.[4]

Once a completed application is certified by the applicant and the nonrefundable payment is successfully processed, CBP officers are to review the application at CBP's Vetting Center to determine whether to conditionally approve the applicant. As part of this vetting process, CBP officers at the Vetting Center are to determine applicants' nationality and admissibility, and assess any potential risk factors. In particular, applicants' information is to be vetted against a number of criminal and terrorist data sets to determine the extent to which applicants may present a risk to the security and safety of the United States. In addition, applicants' information is to be vetted against CBP's TECS to determine what, if any, border violations applicants may have committed in the past that could make them ineligible for participation in a trusted traveler program.[5] Depending on the results of the vetting process, CBP is to conditionally approve or deny applications at the Vetting Center. For applications that are conditionally approved, CBP officers are to update CBP's Global Enrollment System (GES),[6] and applicants are to be notified to schedule an appointment for an interview at a trusted traveler enrollment center.[7] Applicants whose applications are denied are to be notified via e-mail of the denial. Denied applicants can reapply for a trusted traveler program or request reconsideration of the denial to the trusted traveler Ombudsman.[8] If an applicant's reconsideration request is successful, his or her application can be "conditionally approved" and referred to the Vetting Center or an enrollment center and include additional information, such as an applicant's request for reconsideration, for CBP officers to review. For additional information on the Ombudsman reconsideration process, see appendix I. Figure 1 depicts the enrollment process for CBP's trusted traveler programs.

The applicant-vetting process is similar for all four trusted traveler programs; however, there are some differences in the programs' enrollment processes. For example, according to CBP officials, SENTRI applicants from Mexico are required to provide a U.S. address and point of contact, while NEXUS applicants from Canada are not required to provide similar information. CBP officials stated that the requirements are different because, in part, NEXUS applicants from Canada are vetted by their home country and by the United States against a Canadian criminal database, while SENTRI applicants from Mexico are not vetted by their home country. According to CBP officials, Canada sends a "pass" or "fail" notification to CBP following adjudication of an application. If Canada "fails" an application, the United States is to deny the application in all cases. If Canada "passes" an application, the United States is to continue the vetting process and rely on its own determination. These, among other differences, result in the collection of different data for various programs and, according to CBP officials, can have an impact on the amount of time and resources needed to vet individual applicants. More specifically, CBP officers at the Vetting Center told us that it may take more time to review the additional information—U.S. address and point of contact—that is required for SENTRI applicants. This information is used to help CBP determine and assess any potential relationships that could result in the applicant being considered a potential security risk.

In addition, CBP has differences in the rules that govern how CBP officers determine the eligibility of an applicant for each of the trusted traveler programs. For example, CBP uses a different standard when adjudicating—determining eligibility for—a FAST applicant than is used for the other programs.[9] However, CBP officials noted that the commercial environment is different from the passenger environment. More specifically, CBP officials stated that in order to use trusted traveler benefits at a commercial POE, the shipper and carrier have to be Customs-Trade Partnership Against Terrorism (C-TPAT) approved in addition to the driver being a FAST member, a condition that provides an additional layer of security by helping to ensure the shipment is legitimate trade.[10] In addition, there are other variations in the eligibility standards amongst the four programs. For example, a felony conviction disqualifies applicants from joining any of the four trusted traveler programs; however, applicants with misdemeanors may be considered for inclusion in some cases, depending on how recent the convictions were, the overall number of misdemeanor convictions, and the applicant's nationality. For instance, according to CBP officials, FAST applicants may be allowed to enroll in the program with more than one misdemeanor conviction. In addition, CBP honors other countries' and U.S. states' determinations for what crimes constitute a felony, a misdemeanor, or an infraction. For example, a "driving under the influence" charge in one state may be considered an infraction, while in another state it may be considered a misdemeanor.

Once an applicant is conditionally approved, the Vetting Center is to notify the applicant to schedule an interview at an enrollment center. Enrollment centers are located at POEs that have dedicated lanes for trusted travelers, airports with Global Entry kiosks, and other select locations.[11] The interview process requires applicants to meet with a CBP officer at an enrollment center to confirm the accuracy and validity of the information they submitted in their GOES application, provide proof of a valid travel document that is compliant with the Western Hemisphere Travel Initiative (WHTI), submit biometric information to CBP, answer any questions from a CBP officer, and receive a briefing on the trusted traveler programs.[12] In addition, some NEXUS applicants also have to meet with a Canadian Border Services Agency (CBSA) official. During the interview with CBP, applicants are to submit a 10-finger fingerprint that is to be vetted against Federal Bureau of Investigation criminal records, which provide a response within minutes. In addition, applicants' photos are to be taken. As with the vetting and adjudication processes, there are differences in the interview processes for each program. For example, SENTRI applicants who plan to drive across the border must register a vehicle and undergo a vehicle inspection during the interview.

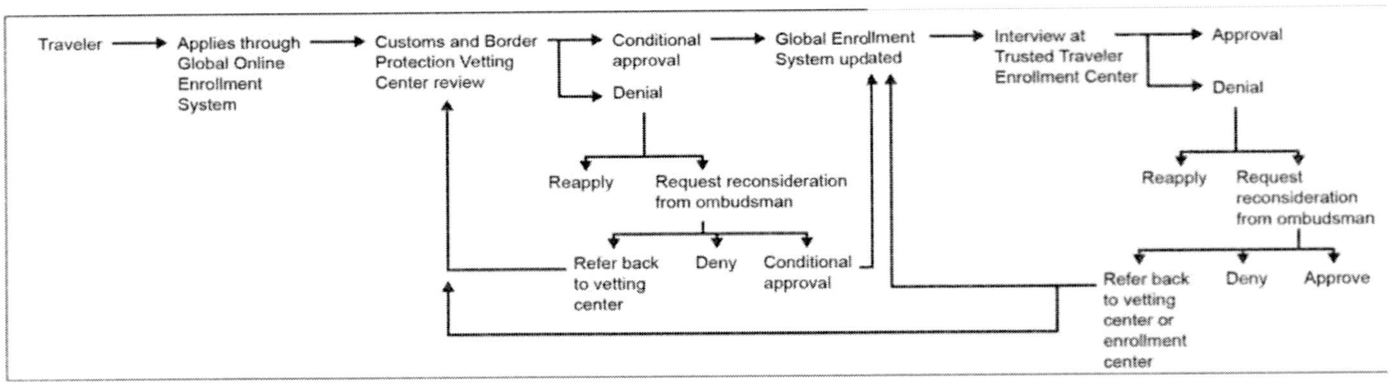

Source: GAO analysis of U.S. Customs and Border Protection information.

Figure 1. U.S. Customs and Border Protection (CBP) Trusted Traveler Enrollment Process.

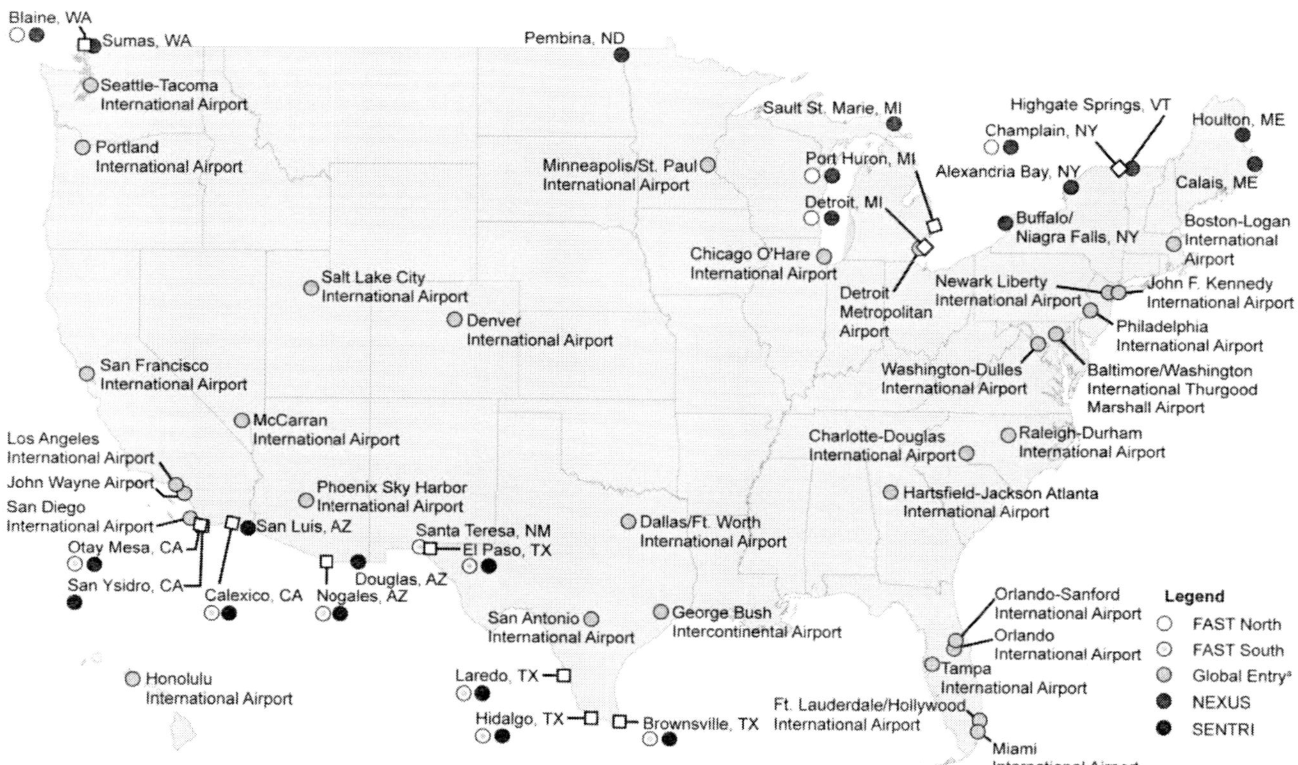

Source: GAO analysis of U.S. Customs and Border Protection data.

Figure 2. Trusted Traveler Ports of Entry (POEs) by Program.

Pending the results of the interview and fingerprint scan at the enrollment center, applicants are approved or denied. If they are approved, CBP is to mail applicants their WHTI-approved trusted traveler card. If denied, applicants have the option to reapply or request reconsideration of the decision through the trusted traveler Ombudsman office. The Ombudsman can uphold a denial or reverse the decision based on the review of an applicant's reconsideration request so that the Vetting Center or enrollment center may consider new or additional information for additional consideration. Once approved, each trusted traveler is to be vetted daily through a "24-hour vetting" process. Under this process, a trusted traveler's information is to be vetted against various databases, including TECS and terrorist data sets, on a daily basis to help ensure that trusted travelers remain low-risk travelers. The 24-hour vetting process that trusted travelers undergo provides an additional layer of screening that regular travelers are not subject to. If a trusted traveler is found to match information in one of the databases CBP screens against during the 24-hour vetting process, the Vetting Center is to review the case and make a determination as to whether the traveler should be allowed to remain in the trusted traveler program.

Trusted Travelers at POEs

When entering the United States through a POE, regular travelers and trusted travelers are generally inspected by a CBP officer at a primary inspection booth.[13] Following the primary inspection, travelers are either permitted to enter the country or referred for additional inspection. Trusted travelers are to receive expedited processing at POEs and use dedicated lanes at POEs. Trusted traveler POE locations that have dedicated lanes for SENTRI, NEXUS, Global Entry, and FAST are shown in figure 2. Of the 328 United States POEs, 65 have dedicated lanes or kiosks for trusted travelers. For a list of POEs with dedicated lanes or kiosks for trusted travelers, see appendix II.

Typically, trusted travelers go through the same inspection process as a regular traveler; however, according to CBP officials, trusted travelers have radio-frequency-identification-enabled trusted traveler cards that are WHTI compliant and automatically populate a CBP officer's computer system at the primary inspection booth. In addition, according to CBP guidance, any trusted traveler that is referred to secondary inspection— when crossing the border— by the CBP officer at the primary inspection booth is to be given "front of line" privileges during his or her secondary inspection. Secondary inspections at land borders generally involve an additional interview with a CBP officer and, if a vehicle is involved, an inspection of the vehicle that can include the use of various inspection methods, such as X-rays and canine inspections. At an airport, secondary inspections can entail additional questioning by a CBP officer and the search of luggage and other items a traveler has with him or her. At commercial trucking POEs, secondary inspection can include referrals to have the truck and its cargo X-rayed, additional questioning, and removal and inspection of cargo.

CBP employs a technique called active lane management to help ensure that trusted travelers' wait times remain lower than those of regular travelers at POEs. More specifically, according to CBP officials, active lane management is used to switch regular traffic lanes to trusted traveler lanes when wait times become too long for trusted travelers, or switch trusted traveler lanes back to regular lanes when the number of trusted travelers coming through the POE requires fewer lanes. CBP officials define wait time as the amount of time it takes a passenger or vehicle to reach the primary inspection booth at the POE from the back of the line. CBP defines inspection time as the amount of time it takes a CBP officer to inspect and release a passenger at the primary inspection booth.

In addition, at Global Entry POEs, trusted travelers scan their passports at a kiosk that allows them to progress past the primary inspection booth without being interviewed by a CBP officer. The kiosk requires travelers to submit their passports, answer a series of questions, have their photos taken, and submit their fingerprints to verify their identities. The answers to the questions and traveler's photo are printed on a receipt. The kiosk also informs the travelers that they have been cleared to enter the country or refers them to secondary inspection. If cleared to enter the country, the trusted traveler has to show a CBP officer his or her passport and the receipt from the kiosk to ensure that the receipt is valid and matches the passenger. At this point, the passenger is allowed to enter the country. If a passenger is referred to secondary inspection, the receipt is to be issued with a large X on it.

Enrollment in Trusted Traveler Programs Has Increased in the Past 5 Fiscal Years; Use Differs by Program and POE

Enrollment in Trusted Traveler Programs Has Increased, Largely because of Growth in Global Entry

As of January 2014, there were about 2.5 million people enrolled in CBP's four trusted traveler programs, and the number of people enrolling in trusted traveler programs has more than quadrupled over the past 5 fiscal years.[14] As shown in figure 3, the number of individuals enrolling in trusted traveler programs has increased from 209,117 in fiscal year 2009 to 857,529 in fiscal year 2013. The growth in enrollments has been largely due to the growth of Global Entry enrollments. CBP officials told us that they believe that the February 2012 announcement that Global Entry members could receive the benefits of the Transportation Security Administration's (TSA) Pre-Check Program, which provides for expedited screening at select TSA checkpoints, contributed to the increase in Global Entry applications. They explained that enrolling in a CBP trusted traveler program was one of the only ways an individual could obtain the Pre- Check benefit from February 2012 through December 2013, since there was not a public application process for Pre-Check prior to December 2013.[15]

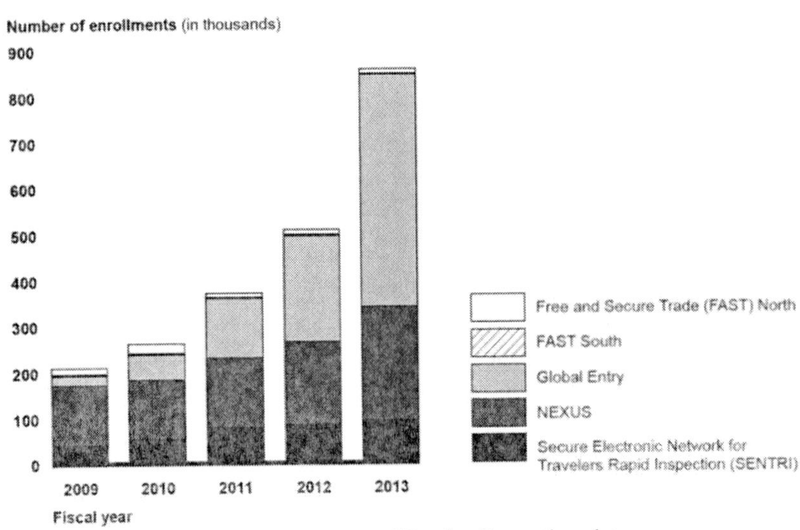

Source: GAO analysis of U.S Customs and Border Protection data.

Note: The number of enrollments includes approved first-time applications, renewal applications, and "reapplications"—the applications of individuals who applied one or more times previously. CBP officials noted that one person may apply to more than one trusted traveler program, so the number of approved applications exceeds the number of trusted travelers.

Figure 3. Trusted Traveler Enrollments, Fiscal Years 2009 through 2013.

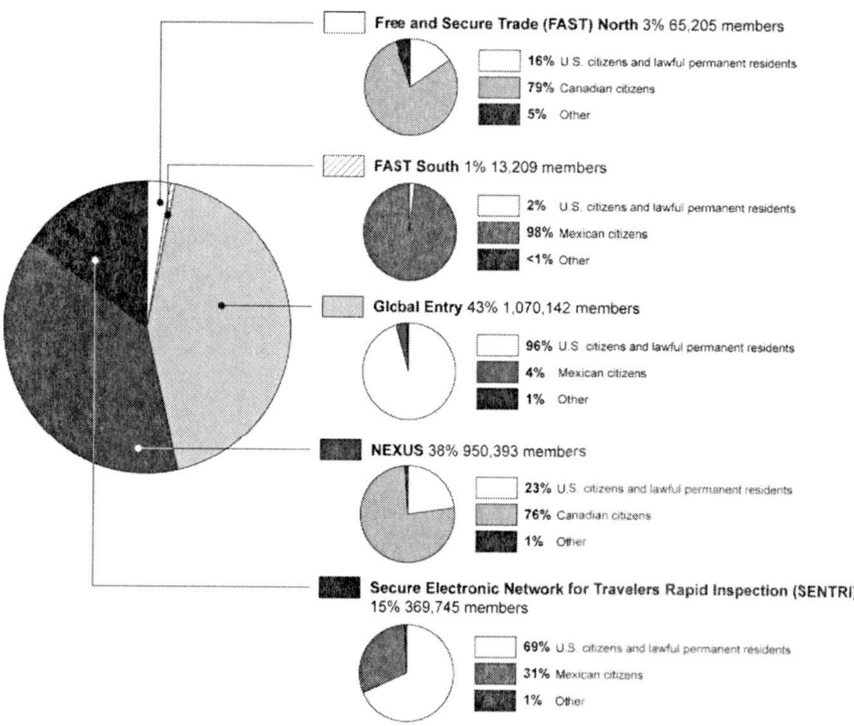

Source: GAO analysis of U.S Customs and Border Protection data.

Note: Membership numbers are as of January 23, 2014. Percentages may not add to 100 because of rounding. The "other" citizenship category for FAST South, Global Entry, and SENTRI includes Canadian citizens, among others. The "other" citizenship category for FAST North and NEXUS includes Mexican citizens, among others. For all programs, the "other" citizenship category may include legal residents of Canada and Mexico who are not citizens of those countries.

Figure 4. Trusted Traveler Membership by Program, as of January 2014.

As of January 2014, most trusted travelers were enrolled in either Global Entry (about 43 percent of all trusted travelers) or NEXUS (about 38 percent of all trusted travelers), as shown in figure 4. The citizenship of trusted travelers varied by program (also shown in figure 4), with U.S. citizens and lawful permanent residents accounting for the largest share of Global Entry and SENTRI memberships, Canadian citizens accounting for the largest share of FAST North and NEXUS memberships, and Mexican citizens accounting for the largest share of FAST South memberships.

CBP officials provided insights on this variation, stating that they have observed that many Canadian citizens live near the border and enroll in NEXUS because they enjoy the benefits of cross-border travel and commerce. They also explained that many Canadians enroll in NEXUS because membership makes them eligible for expedited screening for domestic Canadian flights as well as international flights entering Canada. In addition, they stated that many Mexican and U.S. citizens enroll in SENTRI because they commute across the border for work or to attend school. Further, they said that more Canadian and Mexican truck drivers have enrolled in FAST than have U.S. truck drivers because U.S. truck drivers have opportunities to drive domestic routes, which do not require drivers to cross the border. See appendix III for additional information on trusted traveler application denial rates and revocations from the programs.

Use of Trusted Traveler Programs Has Increased, but Differs by Program and POE

The number of trusted traveler entries increased for all four trusted traveler programs, but the amount of the increase varied by trusted traveler program for fiscal years 2009 through 2013.[16] Border-crossing locations with dedicated SENTRI lanes had the greatest increase in the total number of trusted traveler vehicles entering the United States, increasing from 5.9 million vehicles entering in fiscal year 2009 to 12.6 million vehicles entering in fiscal year 2013. Border-crossing locations with dedicated NEXUS lanes, however, had the greatest growth in terms of percentage increase, with nearly two and a half times as many vehicles entering through dedicated NEXUS lanes in fiscal year 2013 compared with fiscal year 2009 (1.7 million entries in fiscal year 2009 compared with 4 million entries in fiscal year 2013). Global Entry, the newest program, nearly doubled in use from fiscal year 2012 through fiscal year 2013 (1.1 million entries through Global Entry kiosks in fiscal year 2012 compared with 1.9 million entries in fiscal year 2013).[17]

The percentage of entries into the United States that were trusted travelers also differed by program, but was less than 30 percent for all trusted traveler programs. For example, during fiscal year 2013, 3 percent of all travelers that entered through airports that have Global Entry kiosks (1.9 million out of 77 million total entries) were trusted travelers, while 29 percent of all vehicles entering the United States through crossings with SENTRI lanes (12.6 million of 42.9 million total vehicles entries at those crossings) were trusted traveler vehicles. According to CBP officials, SENTRI is the most heavily used trusted traveler program because many SENTRI members cross the southern border frequently, for example, if they live in Mexico but work or attend school in the United States. Figure 5 shows the trends in trusted traveler entries and the percentage of all entries that were trusted traveler entries by program for fiscal years 2009 through 2013.

Within each of the programs, the percentage of travelers entering through trusted traveler lanes varied by individual crossing as well. For example, the percentage of travelers with trusted traveler benefits at crossings with both SENTRI and regular lanes ranged from 0.1 percent to 40 percent in fiscal year 2013.[18] For crossings with both NEXUS and regular lanes, the percentage of travelers with trusted traveler benefits ranged from 0.1 percent at the crossing with the fewest trusted travelers to 34 percent at the crossing with the most trusted travelers in fiscal year 2013.[19] For information on the number of trusted travelers entering the country at each crossing and the percentage of travelers who were trusted travelers in each year, see appendix IV.

CBP Has Designed and Implemented Enrollment Processes, but Opportunities Exist to Enhance Efficiency and Consistency

CBP Could Strengthen Key Areas to Improve the Efficiency of the Application Process

CBP has reported in its trusted traveler guidance the importance of having a reasonable applicant-processing time, and the agency has taken steps to help realize this objective; however, CBP could strengthen three key areas to enhance the efficiency of the application process. These three areas include (1) lack of a performance target for how long it should take to vet an application,

(2) limited interview appointment availability at NEXUS and SENTRI enrollment centers, and (3) lack of systematic data collection on interview appointment availability.

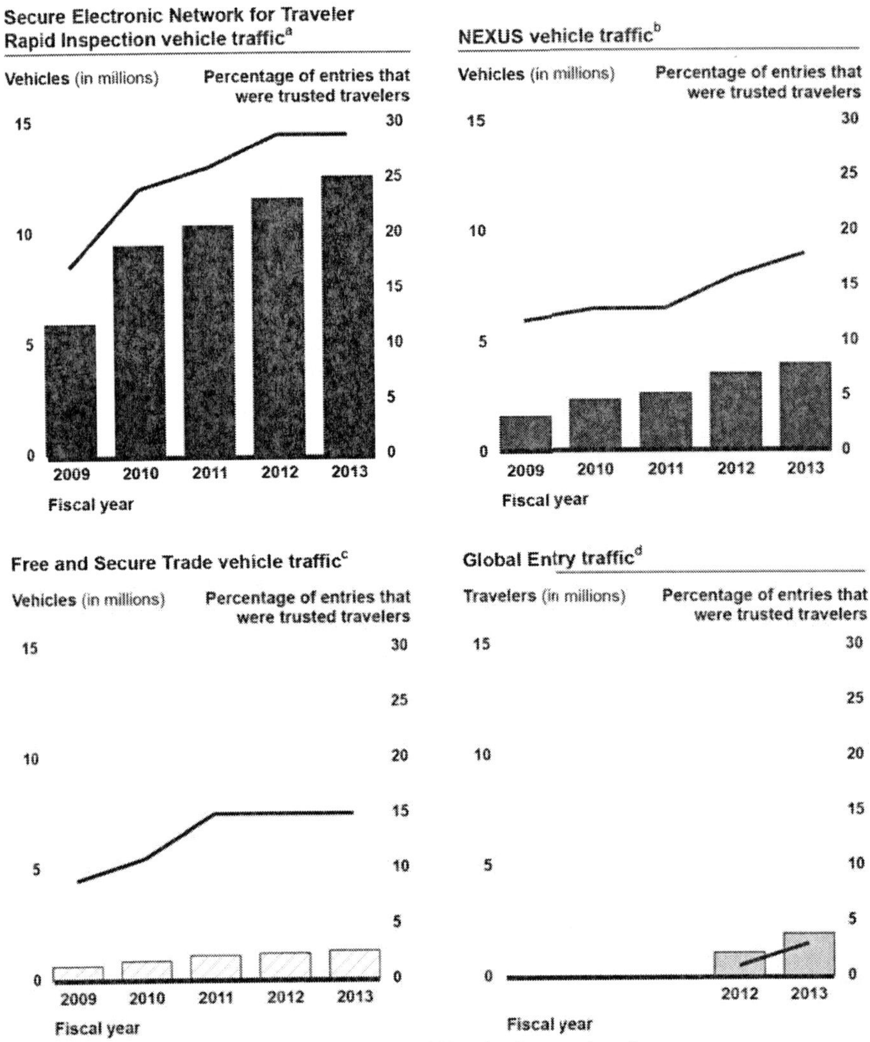

Source: GAO analysis of U.S Customs and Border Protection data.

[a] SENTRI data include only vehicle entries, and do not include travelers entering through pedestrian lanes.

[b] NEXUS data include only NEXUS vehicle entries, and do not include travelers entering through NEXUS air crossings or pedestrians through NEXUS land crossings.

[c] FAST data include entries through dedicated lanes. Drivers who participate in FAST can use their benefits for expedited processing at any crossing.

[d] Global Entry data include the 31 airports in the United States that have Global Entry kiosks available for passengers on inbound international flights. Certain airports in Canada and Ireland have global entry kiosks used by passengers on outbound flights for preclearance for entry into the United States. According to CBP officials, the Canadian preclearance kiosks are used primarily by NEXUS members.

Figure 5. Trends in the Use of Trusted Traveler Lanes and Kiosks, Including the Number of Entries and Percentage of Entries That Were Trusted Travelers, Fiscal Years 2009-2013.

Lack of an application-vetting performance target: CBP did not have a performance target for completing application vetting, as of January 2014. As shown in figure 6, the amount of time between when an initial trusted traveler application is submitted and when the Vetting Center has completed its vetting has varied by program and year, with some programs experiencing vetting times that are longer than others. Notably, the average vetting times for SENTRI applications increased to over 70 days and NEXUS applications increased to about 42 days in fiscal year 2012. In the first 9 months of fiscal year 2013, the vetting times for SENTRI and NEXUS applications decreased, but averaged from 25 through 29 days, or about twice as long as Global Entry applications and three times as long as FAST applications.[20]

In July 2007, CBP established a performance target of having all applications vetted by the CBP Vetting Center within 14 days of receipt. According to a July 2007 memorandum to OFO staff, CBP established this target of 14 days because it recognized the agency should have a plan in place to efficiently process applicants and ensure a reasonable applicant-processing time to meet the expected growth in demand for the trusted traveler programs. However, CBP officials told us that the agency no longer uses the 14-day performance target, as it is not a reasonable target given the current conditions of a high volume of applications and the backlog in interview appointment availability at enrollment centers, which we discuss in more detail later in this report. CBP officials also stated that the agency does not plan to establish a new performance target because it plans to adjust vetting times as needed to take account of current conditions.

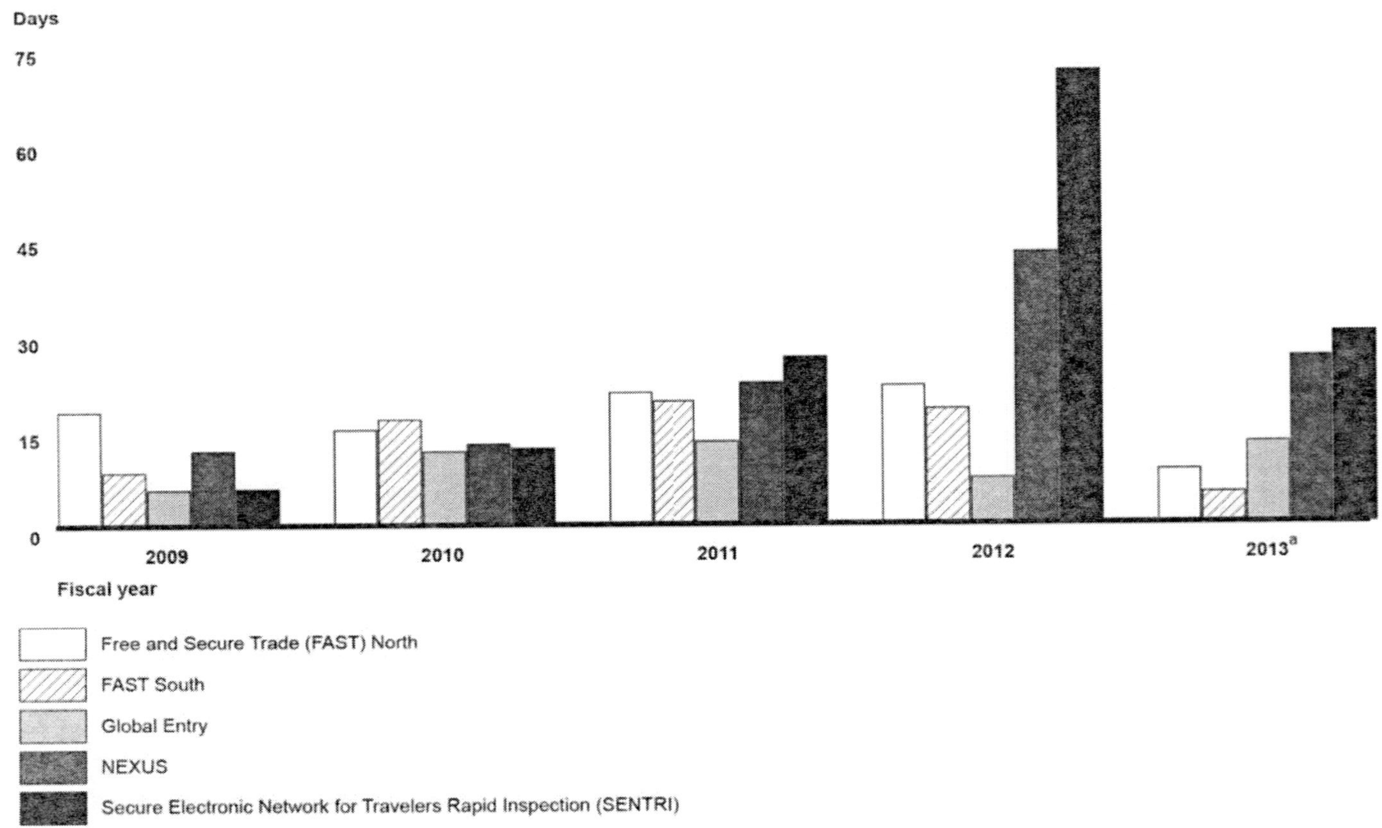

Source: GAO analysis of U.S Customs and Border Protection data.

Notes: The average annual vetting times are for initial applications in which the applicant did not provide information on a vehicle. We reviewed the average vetting times for applications in which the applicant provided information on a vehicle and found they were similar to those in this figure. Applications with information on a vehicle accounted for about 13.8 percent of initial applications from fiscal year 2009 through June 2013.

[a] Fiscal year 2013 data are from October 2012 through June 2013.

Figure 6. Average Trusted Traveler Initial Application Vetting Time, Fiscal Years 2009-2013.

While CBP plans to adjust vetting times as needed, without a performance target or targets for how long vetting should take, CBP is not well positioned to assess how any adjustments in vetting time affect application process times overall or assess progress made in reducing vetting time frames against a target or baseline. Office of Management and Budget guidance states that performance measures should incorporate targets and time frames to help track a program's progress toward reaching its outcome goals—in this case, for example, a reasonable applicant-processing time.[21] In addition, *Standards for Internal Control in the Federal Government* states that managers should compare actual performance against a planned target and analyze significant differences and that performance measures should be monitored and reviewed to validate their propriety.[22] Given changes in the numbers of applications for the different trusted traveler programs over time, setting a performance target for vetting the applications could help better position CBP to assess its processes and timeliness in vetting applications and help make resource allocation decisions. Given the growth of the trusted traveler programs, establishing an updated vetting target and a process for modifying the target as needed, based on factors such as changes in the numbers of applications being filed for the different trusted traveler programs and available resources, consistent with internal control standards, could provide an accountability mechanism to help CBP ensure timely application vetting.

Limited interview appointment availability: CBP's Vetting Center has taken steps to improve the efficiency of the application-vetting process; however, officials in the Vetting Center told us that the limited interview appointment availability for SENTRI and NEXUS applicants has caused the Vetting Center to delay vetting of SENTRI and NEXUS applications.

According to CBP officials, one factor that has affected the Vetting Center's ability to complete vetting of trusted travelers in a timely manner is the growth in trusted traveler applications. The number of applications has more than tripled, from 233,833 in fiscal year 2009 to 895,830 in fiscal year 2013, while the number of CBP officers who vet applications on a full-time basis has slightly increased over that same time period.[23] In fiscal year 2009, there was an average of 23.6 officers vetting applications, and in fiscal year 2013 there was an average of 30.0 officers. Officials stated that the Vetting Center has taken a number of steps over the past 2 years to make the vetting process more efficient and productive. For example, CBP has automated immigration, criminal history, and other background checks and eliminated the need to run manual database queries, provided additional training that reduced the number of supervisor reviews of applications needed, and augmented the Vetting Center workforce by training CBP officers at 24 POEs to vet applications when local traffic allows. As a result of these efforts, Vetting Center officials reported that they have been able to increase the average number of applications vetted per day from 836.9 in fiscal year 2009 to 3,345.1 in fiscal year 2013 and increase the average number of applications each officer vetted per hour from 13.3 in July 2012 to 15.1 in July 2013.

However, despite these productivity gains, the vetting time frames for SENTRI and NEXUS applications have remained relatively long in comparison with vetting time frames for FAST and Global Entry applications. CBP officials stated that the Vetting Center prioritizes Global Entry and FAST applications because of the high volume of Global Entry applications and the importance of FAST membership for trade. Further, Vetting Center officials said that they delay vetting SENTRI and NEXUS applications since they know that SENTRI and NEXUS applicants will not be able to be interviewed in a timely manner because of limited appointment availability at those enrollment centers. NEXUS and SENTRI interviews must be conducted at 1 of the 24 NEXUS enrollment centers or 9 SENTRI enrollment centers because specific enrollment requirements of these programs can be performed only at these locations (i.e., NEXUS applicants must be interviewed by a CBSA officer, and SENTRI applicants must have their cars inspected in order to drive the vehicles in the dedicated lanes). In contrast, Global Entry applicants can schedule an interview at any of the NEXUS and SENTRI enrollment centers or at 1 of the 40 Global Entry enrollment centers. Vetting Center officials explained that the vetting should occur close to the time of the interview so that the vetting results remain current when the enrollment center makes the final decision to approve or deny an application.[24] CBP officials at the Vetting Center told us that as of November 2013, the Vetting Center was vetting SENTRI applications an average of 55 days after they were submitted and NEXUS applications an average of 40 days after they were submitted. In comparison, the officials said that Global Entry applications were vetted 6 days after they were submitted and FAST applications were vetted the same day they were submitted.

In August 2013, there were nearly 33,000 trusted traveler applicants who had not scheduled an interview and another 90,000 applications that were pending vetting at that time. In an effort to streamline the enrollment process and help address this backlog, CBP issued a memorandum in August 2013 instructing enrollment centers to limit the interview to 15 minutes.[25] Prior to this memorandum, interviews were to be no longer than 20 minutes. In addition to this memorandum, CBP officials told us in January 2014 that they eliminated the need for renewal enrollment interviews for current trusted travelers who do not have any derogatory application-vetting results. However, CBP officials at the POEs we visited discussed additional practices they had implemented, or would like to implement, to further improve the efficiency of the interview process, and these officials noted that such practices could be helpful in improving the interview process at other POEs. For example:

- Officials from one POE we visited recommended that CBP eliminate the vehicle examination from the SENTRI enrollment interview and instead inspect the vehicle one of the first few times it crosses the border.[26] This could reduce the interview time and also allow SENTRI applicants to schedule an interview at any of CBP's enrollment centers.
- One enrollment center we visited conducted group briefings on the trusted traveler programs instead of having the CBP officer provide the briefing as part of the one-on-one interview. This allowed some of the CBP officers to start new interviews while another officer briefed all of the approved applicants.
- One enrollment center we visited conducted concurrent CBP-CBSA interviews for NEXUS applicants. According to officials, this reduced the overall interview time because both CBP and CBSA officers ask many of the same questions during the interviews, and by conducting the interview concurrently, the applicant does not have to repeat responses to the same questions.

Standards for program management call for program managers to assess programs on an ongoing basis—taking into account external factors that affect the program, such as growth and resources—to help ensure continued success.[27] According to standards for program management, feasibility studies are one tool program managers can use to determine whether implementing program changes could help mitigate any negative impacts of external factors and achieve organizational goals. Assessing the feasibility could include assessing potential trade-offs, associated costs and benefits, and other factors influencing the ability of enrollment centers to implement additional practices to improve the efficiency of the interview process. CBP officials stated that the agency has continued to delay the vetting of SENTRI and NEXUS applications because of agency priorities and limited appointment availability at enrollment centers and has not assessed the feasibility of implementing additional practices to enhance efficiency, but recognized that there may be opportunities to do so. Given the backlog in enrollment interviews, conducting an assessment of the feasibility of practices implemented or suggested by CBP officials at the POEs we visited, as well as other methods for improving appointment availability, could better position CBP to determine what, if any, additional practices the agency could implement to expedite the interview process. Implementing feasible practices could also better position CBP to achieve its goal of ensuring a reasonable applicant- processing time.

Lack of data on appointment availability over time: CBP monitors appointment availability at each of the enrollment centers on a daily basis, but it does not track appointment availability over time because its enrollment system does not currently have this functionality. As previously discussed, the amount of time it takes for applicants to schedule an interview has an impact on the overall time it takes for applicants to be enrolled in a trusted traveler program. CBP has established a target of having sufficient appointment availability so that every applicant has the potential to be interviewed within 30 days of being conditionally approved by the Vetting Center. However, because CBP does not track data on appointment availability over time, it was not able to provide data on the extent to which it has met this performance target over the past 5 fiscal years.

CBP's daily reports showed that many enrollment centers did not have any available interview appointments in the next 30 days, and some did not have any appointments within the next 90 days. For example, CBP's daily report from March 19, 2013, showed that 21 of the 65 enrollment centers where data were available (about 32 percent) did not have any interview appointments available in the next 30 days, and 99 percent of the interview appointments in that 30-day period were already booked at another 9 enrollment centers (about 14 percent).[28] On that same date, 11 enrollment centers (about 17 percent) did not have any appointments available within the next 90 days, and another 2 enrollment centers had 99 percent of their appointments in that 90-day period booked. At 1 enrollment center, the next available appointment was over 5 months away.

A daily report from January 23, 2014, showed that there may have been some improvement in appointment availability; however, without data on appointment availability over time, CBP cannot determine if this is indicative of a trend or a temporary change in appointment availability. On January 23, 2014, 9 of the 79 enrollment centers where data were available (about 11 percent) did not have any appointments available in the next 30 days, and another 19 enrollment centers (about 24 percent) had 99 percent of their appointments booked in that 30-day period.[29] According to available data, trusted traveler applicants could find it difficult to schedule an interview for the next month at roughly 35 percent of the trusted traveler enrollment centers. Also, on January 23, 2014, 3 enrollment centers (about 4 percent) did not have any appointments available within the next 90 days, and another 9 enrollment centers (about 11 percent) had 99 percent of their appointments booked in that 90-day period. According to available data, trusted traveler applicants could find it difficult to schedule an interview for the next 3 months at roughly 15 percent of the trusted traveler enrollment centers. Depending on where an applicant lives, the lack of appointment availability at specific enrollment centers could result in delaying enrollment for months. On both dates, at least half of the enrollment centers with limited appointment availability for the next 3 months were enrollment centers that process NEXUS applications.

Standards for Internal Control in the Federal Government calls for agency management to track and compare actual performance against goals.[30] Developing a mechanism to track interview appointment availability data over time—rather than on a daily basis—could help CBP determine the extent to which it is meeting its performance target and help it ensure it is taking necessary actions to provide applicants with timely interviews. Further, a mechanism to track appointment availability data could help CBP determine if the steps it has taken to improve the efficiency of the interview process are effective.

CBP Has Processes for Applicant Interviews, but Could Better Ensure They Are Consistently Implemented at Enrollment Centers

CBP has designed some processes for the trusted traveler applicant interview process to help ensure consistency across enrollment centers; however, we found variations in enrollment center interviews and application denial rates, indicating that interviews may not be conducted consistently across enrollment centers. During the enrollment center interview, CBP officers are to collect biometrics, verify documents, and ask applicants questions to help verify the information the applicant provided and determine if the applicant is admissible to the United States and is low risk, based on factors such as criminality and financial solvency, among others. If the Vetting Center has identified derogatory information, then the interviewing CBP officer generally is to ask the applicant to address the issue and then document how this issue was resolved. These processes, as well as a list of suggested interview questions, are documented in CBP's *Trusted Traveler Handbook*. In addition, CBP provides supervisory review of aspects of the interview process conducted at enrollment centers. For example, CBP supervisors are to review all denied applications at enrollment centers, and CBP officials stated that CBP is to conduct a headquarters-level review of all approved applications with derogatory criminal background information. In addition, CBP operates a Self Inspection Program, in which POEs with enrollment centers are to review a sample of interviews to determine if a CBP officer interviewed all applicants, regardless of citizenship or residency; asked the relevant questions; resolved all issues identified by the Vetting Center; and verified the required documents.[31] Further, the Self Inspection Program requires CBP managers to identify and implement corrective actions to address any deficiencies discovered during the assessment. According to CBP, the Self Inspection Program allows CBP leadership to measure the level of compliance with critical operational policies and procedures and examine the issues or underlying causes of noncompliance.

While these processes are designed to help CBP provide oversight of the interview process at its enrollment centers, we identified potential inconsistencies in enrollment centers' interview processes. In particular, during our visits, we observed interviews that did not follow procedures laid out in the *Trusted Traveler Handbook*. For example, we observed interviews at 3 of the 12 enrollment centers we visited, and identified deficiencies with the interviews at 2 of the 3 enrollment centers.[32] Specifically, at 1 NEXUS enrollment center, the CBP officer did not ask any of the interview questions; instead, the applicant was interviewed by a CBSA officer, who is not responsible for establishing admissibility to the United States, and did not ask one of the CBP-suggested questions that are intended to help establish the applicant's admissibility to the United States. At another enrollment center, a CBP officer approved an applicant's enrollment even though the applicant did not have a valid travel document compliant with WHTI, one of the requirements for joining a trusted traveler program. We also reviewed locally developed interview question lists that were used to facilitate the trusted traveler enrollment interviews at 3 enrollment centers that had established such lists and found that they varied and that none of the 3 included all of the suggested interview questions in the *Trusted Traveler Handbook*, which are designed to help establish the applicant's identity, admissibility, and risk level.[33] Specifically, all three lists did not include suggested questions designed to help establish applicants' criminal history, and two of the lists did not include suggested questions designed to help establish applicants' financial solvency. CBP officials noted that while there is not a set list of mandatory questions CBP officers must ask during enrollment interviews, they should ask questions that would allow them to verify the person's identity, admission classification, and risk level. The observations of enrollment interviews and review of locally developed interview question lists from select enrollment centers are not generalizable to all enrollment centers; however, they provided insights and raise questions about the consistency of the interview process across enrollment centers.

Moreover, our analysis of trusted traveler enrollment data from fiscal years 2011 through 2013 indicates that the rate at which trusted traveler applications were denied varied across enrollment centers, as shown in figure 7.[34] Although differences in denial rates across enrollment centers cannot be directly attributed to differences in how centers conduct applicant interviews, data on denial rates can help provide insight into and across the operations of various enrollment centers.

Our analysis of trusted traveler enrollment data shows that the denial rates for FAST North, for example, varied significantly in fiscal year 2013, with 1 enrollment center denying about 16.9 percent of the 537 applicants interviewed at the center, while another enrollment center denied 0.9 percent of the 235 applicants it interviewed. In some years, the denial rates for FAST South, Global Entry, NEXUS, and SENTRI applications also varied significantly. For example,

- the FAST South application denial rate ranged from 0.4 percent of the 489 applications adjudicated at 1 enrollment center to 12.8 percent of the 257 applications adjudicated at another enrollment center in fiscal year 2012,
- the Global Entry application denial rate ranged from 0.1 percent of the 2,767 applications adjudicated at 1 enrollment center to 5.6 percent of the 2,156 applications adjudicated at another enrollment center in fiscal year 2013,
- the NEXUS application denial rate ranged from 0 percent of the 148 applications adjudicated at 1 enrollment center to 6.1 percent of the 343 applications adjudicated at another enrollment center in fiscal year 2011, and

- the SENTRI application denial rate ranged from 0.2 percent of the 1,639 applications adjudicated at 1 enrollment center to 13.6 percent of the 6,350 applications adjudicated at another enrollment center in fiscal year 2012.[35]

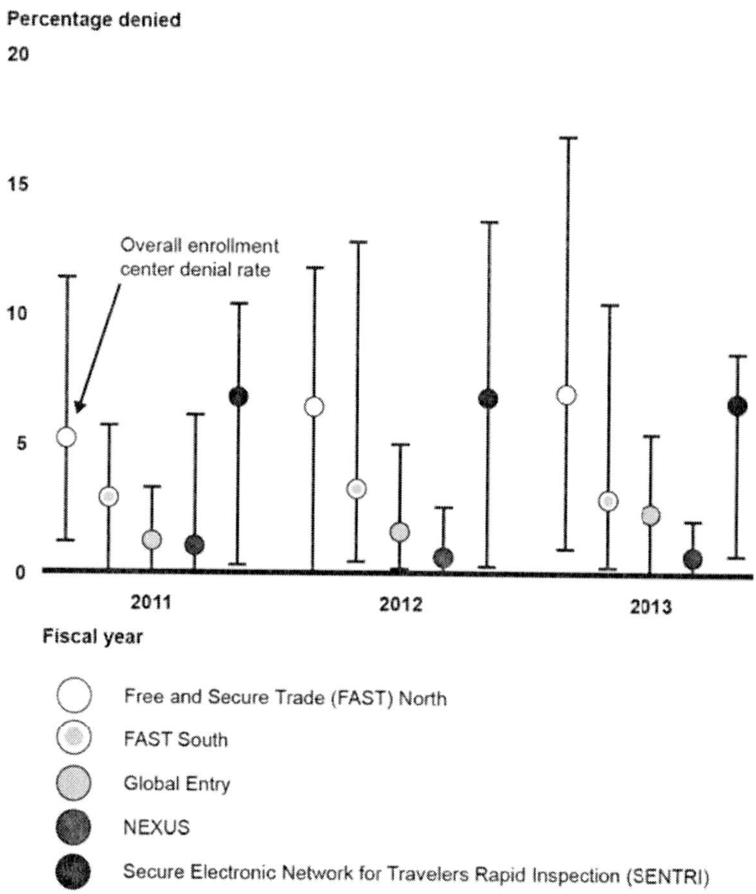

Source: GAO analysis of U.S Customs and Border Protection data.

Note: The range of trusted traveler denial rates includes enrollment centers that adjudicated 100 initial applications or more for that program in the fiscal year. The overall enrollment center denial rate was calculated by dividing the number of initial applications denied at all enrollment centers by the total number of initial applications adjudicated by enrollment centers.

Figure 7. Range of Trusted Traveler Application Denial Rates at Enrollment Centers.

Furthermore, 7 enrollment centers had the highest or lowest denial rates in more than 1 fiscal year. For example, from fiscal years 2011 through 2013,1 enrollment center consistently had the highest FAST South denial rates, and 1 enrollment center consistently had the lowest FAST South denial rates. In addition, 1 enrollment center had the lowest NEXUS denial rates from fiscal years 2011 through 2013.

We recognize that differences in denial rates across enrollment centers can be attributable to various factors. For example, according to CBP officials, differences in the applicant populations that go to certain enrollment centers or differences in the experience levels of the CBP officers conducting interviews may have contributed to differences across enrollment centers. However, given that denials are based at least in part on interviews conducted at enrollment centers, the variation in denial rates could indicate that the interview process may result in different outcomes across enrollment centers.

While CBP has processes to help provide oversight of the interview process at enrollment centers, including supervisory reviews and a Self Inspection Program, CBP's GES, the trusted traveler system of record, does not document the questions CBP officers ask or the applicants' responses, hindering the level of oversight provided through CBP's existing processes. For example, according to CBP officials, the headquarters-level review helps to ensure that the background checks for a select number of approved applicants did not find potentially disqualifying information, but it does not take into account admissibility issues or all risk factors discussed during the interview, as these may not be documented.[36] Similarly, since interview questions and responses are not documented, the supervisory review of denied applications does not provide supervisors with full information on the applicant or allow supervisors to help ensure that CBP officers are asking all relevant questions. Moreover, neither of these processes provides oversight over the majority of applications, which are approved and do not have the type of derogatory background investigation findings that would trigger a headquarters-level review. CBP's internal inspection process requires a review of a random sampling of applications, which could help CBP monitor the implementation of the interview process across enrollment centers and potentially review both approved and denied applications. However, because GES does not document the questions CBP officers ask or the applicants' responses to these questions, it would be difficult for CBP, as a part of its internal self-inspection, to determine whether the questions asked were sufficient to determine whether the applicant was low risk or whether the applicant's responses support the final adjudication decision.

Standards for Internal Control in Federal Government calls for agencies to clearly document internal control transactions so that managers can examine and use the information to make decisions and monitor programs.[37] CBP officials stated that they did not want to include a set list of questions in GES and require CBP officers to document responses to these questions because they want CBP officers to be able to cater the interview questions to the specific applicant. We recognize that there is value in allowing CBP officers to vary the questions they ask based on the applicant and that documenting all interview questions and responses could require use of more resources at enrollment centers. However, establishing a mechanism or mechanisms in GES so that CBP officers could efficiently document the kinds of questions they asked and the nature of the applicants' responses where appropriate, for example, by using check boxes to indicate which of a prepopulated set of questions and responses apply, could help minimize any resource impacts. Furthermore, such a mechanism or mechanisms could better position CBP to monitor the interview process through its other existing processes, such as the Self Inspection Program, to help ensure that interviews are being conducted consistently and in accordance with its policies at enrollment centers.

CBP Could Better Ensure That Foreign Adjudication Procedures Are Documented

CBP has implemented bilateral arrangements with 9 countries, and DHS has signed bilateral arrangements with 3 additional countries that document the countries' intent to explore implementing joint trusted traveler programs.[38] The bilateral arrangements allow foreign citizens from these respective countries to enroll in the Global Entry program and enter the United States through expedited lanes at aviation POEs.[39] CBP has documented operating procedures for vetting or sharing information on applicant-vetting results for 2 of these 12 countries and CBP officials have stated that the agency plans to add separate appendixes on each country when updating its Global Entry standard operating procedures. However, CBP officials told us that these appendixes will provide general statements about operating procedures, and as CBP is in the process of updating the standard operating procedures, it is too early to tell what information will be included in the country-specific appendixes.

The bilateral arrangements with 8 of the remaining 10 countries that do not have documented operational procedures state that CBP and the partner country plan to work together to develop and document operational procedures. As an example, the bilateral arrangement with one country that was signed by both countries in April 2011 states that "additional Initiative requirements and qualifications, procedures for communication and vetting, and other operational details concerning the implementation of the Initiative are expected to be set forth in a written joint operational program plan." However, according to CBP officials, documenting foreign countries' operational plans or procedures would be burdensome and would not add value, as these plans would not be legally binding. Further, officials stated that the language in the bilateral arrangements does not necessarily indicate a standard operating procedure would be documented.

However, CBP has recognized the importance of understanding the foreign countries' procedures. CBP officials told us that during the meetings that lead up to the bilateral arrangements, DHS or CBP communicates the trusted traveler eligibility criteria and discusses the kinds of information that the other country is to review as part of its vetting process to help ensure that partner countries apply the same standards that the United States does when vetting applicants. Furthermore, after an arrangement is signed, CBP officials stated that there are numerous follow-up conversations between CBP and the foreign country to determine which individuals will be eligible to apply, how those applications will be submitted, and how a foreign country will communicate its vetting of applicants. CBP officials noted that because each country has different laws, databases, and resources, there are some differences in how the trusted traveler programs are implemented in each country. For example, CBP revets trusted travelers every 24 hours to help ensure their continued eligibility, while, according to CBP officials, other countries may choose to revet their citizens on an annual basis. Additionally, CBP stated that it holds regular meetings with partner countries to help ensure the integrity of the program and that operations are running appropriately. However, CBP has not documented the results of these discussions, and thus the knowledge of the other countries' operational procedures is maintained by those CBP and DHS officials who participated in the meetings.

Standards for Internal Control in the Federal Government states that detailed and appropriate documentation is a key component of internal controls and allows stakeholders to make effective decisions about programs or operations.[40] While CBP officials have stated that conducting additional meetings with each partner country to jointly develop bilateral operational plans and procedures is overly burdensome, CBP could document the operational procedures it has already discussed with each partner country in its planned update of the Global Entry standard operating procedures, or elsewhere. Such operational procedures may include the databases or types of information the foreign country will use to vet applicants, how often the foreign country will revet trusted travelers to ensure continued eligibility, and how information on applicants' and trusted travelers' eligibility will be shared, for example. Without such documentation, there is no institutional record that those countries' procedures for vetting applicants help to ensure that only low-risk applicants are enrolled.

CBP Moves Trusted Travelers through POEs More Quickly than Other Travelers, Allowing CBP to Focus Its Resources on Travelers It Knows Less About

Trusted Traveler Wait Times Are Shorter than Wait Times for Regular Travelers and Differ by Program and Port of Entry

Trusted travelers generally experience shorter average wait times for primary inspections than regular traffic at crossings for all four trusted traveler programs.[41] Our analysis of CBP data indicates that passenger vehicles crossing the southern border generally experience the greatest benefits from the trusted traveler programs; however, concerns about the reliability of wait time data prevented us from directly comparing average wait times from crossing to crossing.[42] According to CBP officials, wait times are generally longer along the southern border than along the northern border. Our analysis of CBP wait time data showed that at 11 out of 14 crossings with SENTRI lanes, regular traveler vehicles waited at least 15 minutes longer on average than trusted traveler vehicles in fiscal year 2013.[43] At 5 of those 11 crossings, vehicles in regular traffic lanes waited at least 30 minutes longer on average than vehicles in trusted traveler lanes. The crossing with a SENTRI lane with the greatest difference in wait times had an estimated difference between the average trusted traveler wait time and the average regular traffic wait time of over 1 hour.[44] Along the northern land border, crossings with NEXUS lanes generally had more similar wait times for trusted and regular travelers.[45]

Specifically, our analysis of CBP wait time data showed that at 15 of 18 crossings with NEXUS lanes, regular travelers waited less than 15 minutes longer than trusted travelers on average in fiscal year 2013.[46] Trusted travelers also experienced somewhat shorter wait times in airports on average. Our analysis of CBP wait time data showed that regular travelers waited an estimated 10 to 27 minutes longer on average than trusted travelers at the 31 airports in the United States with Global Entry kiosks in fiscal year 2013.

Among commercial traffic, our analysis of CBP data showed FAST participants generally experienced slightly shorter wait times than regular traffic on average. FAST participants spent less time waiting on average than regular commercial traffic at 12 of 15 crossings with FAST lanes in fiscal year 2013; however, this difference was less than 15 minutes on average at all but one of these crossings. For the other 3 crossings with FAST lanes, the average wait time for FAST lanes was between about 30 seconds and 8 minutes longer than for regular lanes. Some crossings with FAST lanes report longer estimated average wait times for FAST traffic because of the high number of program members and factors unique to specific crossings. For example, during our visit to one FAST North crossing, CBP officials told us that they had a pilot project in which Canada was prescreening FAST trucks, which was causing delays in the FAST lane. In addition, according to CBP officials, infrastructure constraints at certain POEs can lead to increased wait times for FAST members. For example, at some POEs, the dedicated FAST lanes are separated by barriers from regular lanes, and drivers must commit to either FAST lanes or regular lanes before they can see which set of lanes has a shorter queue. CBP officials told us that most of the benefits derived from being a FAST member are realized during the secondary inspection process, which provides FAST members "front of line" privileges when referred for additional inspection.

Figure 8 shows our analysis of the number of crossings by program with different categories of wait time differences for trusted and regular travelers in fiscal year 2013.

CBP manages lanes operating as dedicated lanes at land crossings with trusted traveler lanes in order to keep trusted traveler wait times as low as possible. At airports, trusted travelers undergo primary inspection through kiosks rather than with a CBP officer. CBP officials told us that they can use wait times for Global Entry kiosks to help them prioritize decisions as to where they should deploy additional Global Entry kiosks.

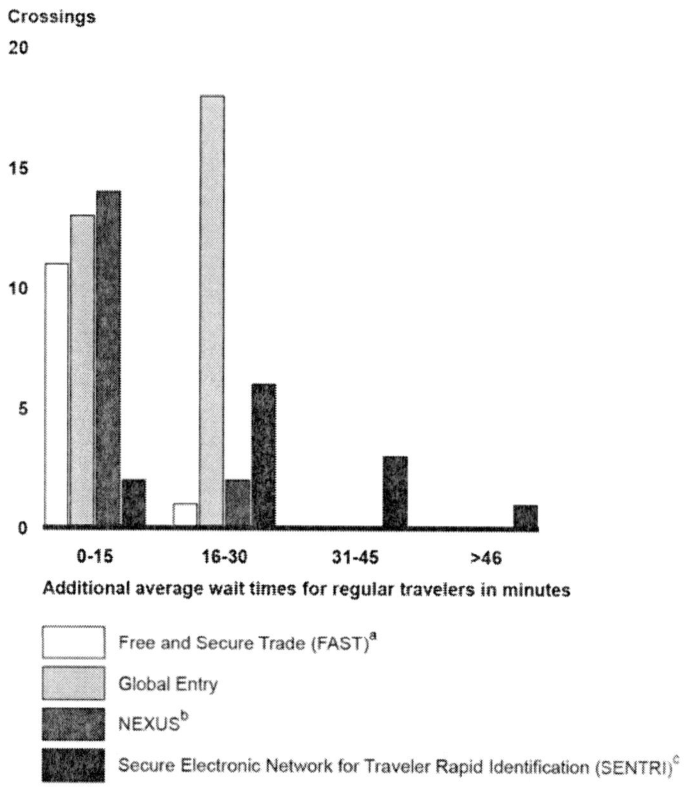

Source: GAO analysis of U.S. Customs and Border Protection data.

[a] At 3 FAST crossings, trusted travelers waited longer on average than regular travelers.

[b] One NEXUS crossing has only trusted traveler lanes, and is therefore not included in the figure.

[c] One SENTRI crossing had only regular lanes in fiscal year 2013 and another had only trusted traveler lanes. These 2 crossings are not included in the figure.

Figure 8. Number of Border Crossings with Differences in Wait Times for Trusted and Regular Travelers by Program, Fiscal Year 2013.

According to CBP officials, CBP has a goal of keeping trusted traveler wait times to less than 15 minutes at crossings with SENTRI or NEXUS lanes, and uses active lane management to switch regular traffic lanes to trusted traveler lanes when wait times become too long for trusted travelers. Infrastructure variations at some POEs, however, limit CBP's ability to reduce wait times for trusted travelers because passenger and commercial trusted traveler vehicles may have to wait in regular traffic lanes before they are able to access dedicated lanes. For example, according to CBP officials, at one northern border vehicle crossing, NEXUS members are not able to enter NEXUS lanes until after a choke point, and if the regular traffic line is backed up past that choke point, NEXUS members have to wait with the regular traffic until they are able to access the NEXUS lanes. Commercial traffic faces the same types of infrastructure variations. At one northern vehicle crossing, FAST members have to wait with regular passenger traffic until they are able to access the FAST lanes. CBP has undertaken efforts to expand infrastructure at specific POEs in an effort to mitigate these concerns. For example, CBP began expanding the San Ysidro, California, POE, which is the busiest passenger POE in the nation.

Figure 9 shows the choke point at the Detroit POE, where trusted traveler traffic, including NEXUS and FAST traffic, may have to wait with regular traffic before being allowed to access the NEXUS and FAST lanes.

Trusted Travelers Are Inspected More Quickly and Commit Fewer Violations than Regular Travelers, Allowing CBP to Focus Its Resources on Other Travelers

Inspections of trusted travelers at the primary inspection booths are generally shorter than inspections of regular travelers, and according to the *Trusted Traveler Handbook*, the average primary inspection per passenger vehicle in dedicated lanes should not exceed 30 seconds per vehicle. Our analysis of CBP data showed that CBP met this goal at 12 of 14 crossings with SENTRI lanes and 12 of 18 crossings with NEXUS lanes in fiscal year 2013.[47] In regular traffic lanes, the average inspection time was longer. Our analysis of CBP data showed that primary inspections took about twice as long or longer on average for regular travelers than for trusted travelers at 11 of 14 crossings with SENTRI lanes and 11 of 18 crossings with NEXUS lanes in fiscal year 2013.[48] On average, CBP officers spent up to five times as long inspecting regular travelers at crossings with SENTRI lanes and up to three times as long inspecting regular travelers at crossings with NEXUS lanes. These inspection times ranged from 48 seconds to 97 seconds at crossings with SENTRI lanes and 23 seconds to 64 seconds at crossings with NEXUS lanes in that same year, according to CBP data. Trusted travelers are prescreened against multiple databases as part of their enrollment in the program; therefore, according to CBP officials, the agency can inspect them more efficiently at crossings, which allows CBP officers to focus more resources on travelers they know less about. For example, at the busiest crossing with SENTRI lanes, the average inspection time was 25 seconds for trusted travelers and 68 seconds for regular travelers in fiscal year 2013. At that crossing, a single CBP officer could inspect up to 53 regular vehicles in 1 hour; however, that same CBP officer could inspect up to 144 SENTRI vehicles in the same amount of time. According to CBP officials, prioritizing resources is one of the goals of the trusted traveler program. According to CBP data, the four trusted traveler programs saved over 270,000 CBP officer hours at primary inspection booths at POEs in fiscal year 2013. According to CBP data, this savings in CBP officer time equates to approximately $15.5 million in avoided costs.

In addition to determining that trusted travelers take less time to inspect than regular travelers, our analysis of CBP data indicates that trusted travelers commit fewer border violations, such as smuggling, than regular travelers. Our analysis of CBP data shows that the majority of violations result from CBP seizing illegal goods such as drugs, excess currency, or undeclared merchandise; however, some violations result from nonseizure arrests such as if a person with a warrant for a non-border- related crime attempts to enter the country. CBP identifies violations after sending travelers from primary inspection to secondary inspection, either randomly or based on the suspicion of the CBP officer at the primary inspection booth. CBP uses algorithms to determine which travelers are randomly sent for secondary inspection, as well as changing criteria that are used to randomly select travelers for secondary inspections. For example, CBP can target vehicles or travelers based on specific categories or criteria, such as age, that are then relayed to CBP officers at the primary inspection booths with little to no notice. CBP officers can also use their professional discretion to refer any travelers to secondary inspection that they may deem to be potential risks. Both trusted and regular travelers are subject to secondary inspection based on suspicion and random referral, and CBP calculated the rate at which travelers commit violations by calculating the percentage of people who are sent to secondary inspection that are found to have committed violations. Our analysis of CBP data indicates that trusted travelers commit violations at a lower rate than general travelers, and while these rates are not directly comparable because of differences in the secondary referral processes for trusted and regular travelers, the variation in the rates is notable. Specifically, our analysis of CBP data showed that of those travelers sent for secondary inspection, approximately 1 out of every 140 regular travelers was found to have committed a violation; whereas less than 1 out of every 3,000 trusted travelers was found to have committed a violation in fiscal year 2013.

Trusted travelers at land POEs had been randomly referred to secondary inspection at a higher rate than regular travelers, according to CBP officials; however, CBP took steps in 2013 to reduce the likelihood of trusted travelers at land POEs being referred to secondary inspection more often than regular travelers. The random referral rate of trusted travelers is based on a set of rules specific to trusted travelers that targets both individuals and vehicles. For regular travelers, CBP uses a program called Compliance Examination (COMPEX), which randomly selects regular travelers entering the country for more detailed inspections. CBP officers at land POEs we visited told us that their POEs used both the trusted traveler random referral system and COMPEX in lanes dedicated for SENTRI or NEXUS. CBP officials told us that they have adjusted this and now use COMPEX only in the regular traveler lanes. The removal of COMPEX in trusted traveler lanes at land POEs should reduce the rate at which trusted travelers entering the country through a dedicated trusted traveler lane are referred to secondary inspection. However, CBP officers at two POEs we visited along the southern border (San Ysidro and Otay Mesa) told us that most trusted travelers who are sent to secondary inspection spend less time getting through the port than a regular traveler using a regular lane who is not referred to secondary inspection.

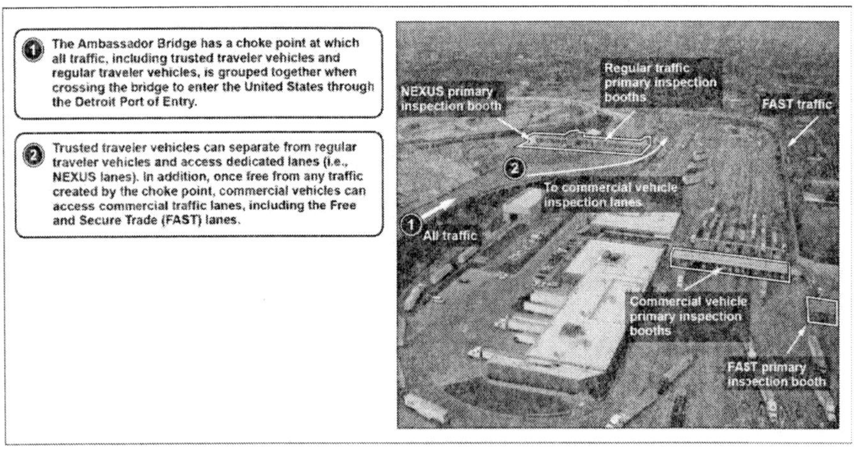

Source: GAO analysis of U.S. Customs and Border Protection officials statements and photograph.

Figure 9. Detroit Port of Entry Choke Point at Which Trusted Traveler Traffic May Wait with Regular Traffic.

When travelers, including trusted travelers, are caught committing violations, CBP has a goal to prosecute offenders to the full extent of the law. For all instances of participants caught smuggling in dedicated lanes, CBP disseminates a press release, unless doing so would compromise an ongoing investigation. For example, on January 22, 2014, CBP issued a press release regarding a trusted traveler who had failed to truthfully declare approximately $6,000 worth of merchandise, and was assessed a $6,000 penalty. According to the *Trusted Traveler Handbook*, CBP is to inform applicants of the consequences of a border violation by a trusted traveler during his or her enrollment. CBP officials noted that the potential loss of the benefit is one of the most effective deterrents to such activity. CBP identifies trusted traveler border violations during the daily vetting process and uses this information to determine whether a trusted traveler should be allowed to remain in the program or whether the traveler should have the benefit revoked.

CONCLUSION

Trusted traveler programs are a key component of CBP's risk-based approach to facilitate travel and trade coming through U.S. POEs while keeping out terrorists and their weapons and enforcing U.S. laws and regulations, including those that prevent the illegal entry of persons and contraband. According to CBP, its trusted traveler programs help it achieve this dual mission by allowing it to focus resources at the POEs on passengers and cargo that have not been identified as low risk. CBP has recognized the importance of processing trusted traveler applications in a reasonable time frame and has taken some steps to help improve the efficiency of the enrollment process. CBP could better ensure the timeliness of its enrollment process by establishing an updated performance target for vetting applications and a process to modify the target as needed based on factors such as application volume and resources, assessing the feasibility of practices to expedite the interview process and implementing feasible practices, and developing a mechanism to track interview appointment availability data over time. Further, the success of the trusted traveler programs is predicated on enrolling low-risk travelers, allowing CBP to focus its resources on travelers it knows less about. CBP has established processes to interview applicants; however, establishing mechanisms for CBP officers to efficiently document the types of questions they asked and the nature of applicants' responses, when appropriate, in GES could allow CBP to better monitor the interview process through its other existing processes, such as the Self Inspection Program. This could help ensure that the interview process is being conducted consistently and in accordance with CBP policies across enrollment centers. Furthermore, without documentation on all partner countries' vetting procedures—such as the databases or types of information the foreign country will use to vet applicants, how often the foreign country will revet trusted travelers, and how information on applicants' and trusted travelers' eligibility will be shared—there is no institutional record that those countries' procedures for vetting applicants help to ensure that only low-risk applicants are enrolled.

RECOMMENDATIONS FOR EXECUTIVE ACTION

To help assess and improve the timeliness of the trusted traveler application adjudication process, we recommend that the Commissioner of CBP take the following three actions:

- establish an updated performance target for completing application vetting and a process to modify that target, as needed, based on factors such as changes in the number of trusted traveler program applications and available resources;
- assess the feasibility of practices to expedite the interview process, which could include assessing the potential trade-offs, costs, and benefits associated with any proposed practices, such as those currently proposed or implemented at specific enrollment centers, and implement those practices CBP determines to be feasible; and
- develop a mechanism to track enrollment interview appointment availability data over time.

To better ensure that the trusted traveler eligibility criteria and applicant adjudication processes are consistently implemented in accordance with CBP policy at all enrollment centers and by partner countries, we recommend that the Commissioner of CBP take the following two actions:

- establish a mechanism or mechanisms in GES to allow CBP officers to efficiently document the types of interview questions asked and the nature of applicant responses, when appropriate, and then use this information to monitor the implementation of the interview process, and

- document information CBP has obtained on the operational procedures, such as those used to vet and share information on applicants, of foreign countries that have signed bilateral arrangements with the United States to participate in trusted traveler programs.

AGENCY COMMENTS AND OUR EVALUATION

We provided a draft of this report to DHS for review and comment. DHS provided written comments, which are summarized below and technical comments, which we incorporated as appropriate. DHS concurred with four of the five recommendations in the report and described actions underway or planned to address them. DHS did not concur with one recommendation in the report.

With regard to the first recommendation, that CBP establish an updated performance target for completing application vetting, DHS concurred and stated that CBP OFO will work with the trusted traveler Vetting Center to establish an updated performance target, identify factors that may impact the target, and identify the process to modify the target based on these factors. DHS stated that its initial assessment is to be completed by August 2014 and provided a final completion date of October 2014. These planned actions, if fully implemented, should address the intent of the recommendation.

With regard to the second recommendation, that CBP assess the feasibility of practices to expedite the interview process and implement those practices CBP determines to be feasible, DHS concurred and stated that CBP OFO plans to conduct site visits at 5 to 10 enrollment centers to identify best practices, test and evaluate those practices in other enrollment centers, and then implement relevant practices at other enrollment centers, as appropriate. DHS provided an estimated completion date of November 2014. These planned actions, if fully implemented, should address the intent of the recommendation.

With regard to the third recommendation, that CBP develop a mechanism to track enrollment interview appointment data availability over time, DHS concurred and stated that by August 2014, CBP OFO will determine the modifications that would need to be made to GOES to implement this recommendation. DHS stated that subsequent milestones for implementation and completion dates will be finalized, as appropriate, with a final estimated completion date of December 2014. If fully implemented, these actions should address the intent of the recommendation.

With regard to the fourth recommendation, that CBP establish a mechanism in GES to allow CBP officers to efficiently document the types of interview questions asked and the nature of applicant responses, when appropriate, and use this information to monitor the implementation of the interview process, DHS did not concur. DHS stated that the interview process for trusted traveler programs is equivalent to a border crossing inspection. During the interview, as well as an inspection, DHS stated that CBP officers must make a determination of an applicant's identity, nationality, and admissibility. DHS stated that the burden of proof is on the applicant to establish that he or she is not inadmissible to the United States, and the criterion at the end of the interaction is that the applicant has overcome the burden of proof and the CBP officer is satisfied that the applicant is admissible. Further, DHS stated that there are no scripted questions that must be asked and that when a CBP officer approves an applicant, it is implicit that the officer was satisfied as to the identity, nationality, and admissibility of the applicant. DHS also stated that creating a measure for this process would force a line of questioning and additional steps that may not be relevant for most applicants and the additional step to "capture" this information would add to the time required to complete the interview. DHS noted that questions and answers relating to the risk and eligibility of a trusted traveler, beyond those in the inspection process, can already be documented in the comments section of GES.

We continue to believe that CBP should establish a mechanism in GES to allow CBP officers to efficiently document the types of interview questions asked and the nature of applicant responses, when appropriate, and use this information to monitor the implementation of the interview process. The intent of the trusted traveler programs is to provide expedited travel for preapproved, low risk travelers through dedicated lanes and kiosks. Through the application vetting and interview process, CBP officers are to ensure that the applicants are low-risk, in addition to making a determination about an applicant's identity, nationality, and admissibility.

As noted in the report, we identified potential inconsistencies in enrollment centers' interview processes, including instances where CBP officers did not follow procedures laid out in the *Trusted Traveler Handbook*. For example, we observed interviews at 3 of the 12 enrollment centers we visited, and identified deficiencies with the interviews at 2 of the 3 enrollment centers. Specifically, we observed one interview where a CBP officer did not ask any of the interview questions suggested in the *Trusted Traveler Handbook*; rather, the applicant was interviewed separately by a CBSA officer who was not responsible for establishing an applicant's admissibility to the United States. We also found that 3 enrollment centers had established lists of questions that were used by CBP officers at those centers during the interview process and that the three interview question lists were different and that none of the three included all of the suggested interview questions in the *Trusted Traveler Handbook*, which are designed to help establish the applicant's identity, admissibility, and risk level. In addition, we found significant variation in denial rates across enrollment centers. As noted in our report, while differences in denial rates across enrollment centers can be attributable to various factors, given that denials are based at least in part on interviews conducted at enrollment centers, the variation in denial rates could indicate that the interview process may result in different outcomes across enrollment centers.

Further, this recommendation is not intended to imply that CBP should develop a set of scripted questions for trusted traveler program interviews or add more time to the interview process. Rather, as stated in the report, we recognize that there is value in allowing CBP officers to vary the questions they ask based on the applicant and that documenting all interview questions and responses could require use of more resources at enrollment centers. However, as we stated in the report, we believe that establishing a mechanism or mechanisms in GES so that CBP officers could efficiently document the kinds of questions they asked and the nature of the applicants' responses where appropriate, could help minimize any resource impacts. CBP officers are not required to use the comments sections in GES to consistently record the types of questions asked and the nature of applicant responses in those comments. Further, allowing comments to be entered into GES does not place a control over the interview process to ensure that CBP officers are asking questions pertaining to an applicant's identity, nationality, and admissibility, and to ensure the applicant's low-risk status. CBP could accomplish this by, for example, using check boxes to indicate which of a prepopulated set of questions and responses apply, as we noted in the report. Moreover, a mechanism or mechanisms to efficiently document the kinds of questions asked and the nature of responses could better position CBP to monitor the interview process through its other existing processes, such as the Self Inspection Program, to help ensure that interviews are being conducted consistently and in accordance with its policies at enrollment centers. For example, CBP's Self Inspection Program requires POEs with enrollment centers to report whether a CBP officer "asked the mandatory questions" during the interview process. However, as noted in the report, because GES does not document the questions CBP officers ask or the applicants' responses to these questions, it would be difficult for CBP, as a part of its internal self-inspection, to determine whether the questions asked were sufficient to determine whether the applicant was low risk or whether the applicant's responses support the final adjudication decision. When appropriate, documenting the types of questions—for example, pertaining to the applicant's identity, nationality, admissibility, and risk factors—that were asked during the interview and the nature of applicant responses—for example, confirmation that the identity, nationality, admissibility, and low-risk status were verified by the CBP officer—could help provide CBP with assurances that CBP officers are following the procedures and guidelines laid out in the *Trusted Traveler Handbook*. Thus, we continue to believe that this recommendation is valid and CBP should take action to fully implement it.

With regard to the fifth recommendation, that CBP document information CBP has obtained on the operational procedures, such as those used to vet and share information on applicants, of foreign countries that have signed bilateral agreements with the United States to participate in trusted traveler programs, DHS concurred. DHS stated that CBP OFO has drafted an update to the Global Entry Standard Operating Procedure that is currently under review and is expected to address the operational procedures of foreign countries that have signed bilateral arrangements with the United States. DHS stated that the estimated completion date is August 2014. This planned action should address the intent of the recommendation.

Rebecca Gambler
Director, Homeland Security and Justice

APPENDIX I. OMBUDSMAN RECONSIDERATION PROCESS

Individuals that are denied enrollment in a trusted traveler program or revoked from a program have the option to request reconsideration of the decision through the trusted traveler Ombudsman office. The Ombudsman may consider additional information and can uphold a denial or revocation or reverse the decision. From fiscal year 2009 through 2013, the Ombudsman reviewed 24,363 cases and overturned denials or revocations in approximately 43 percent of the cases. As shown in figure 10, the number of cases the Ombudsman reviewed nearly tripled from 2,596 in fiscal year 2009 to 7,449 in fiscal year 2013.

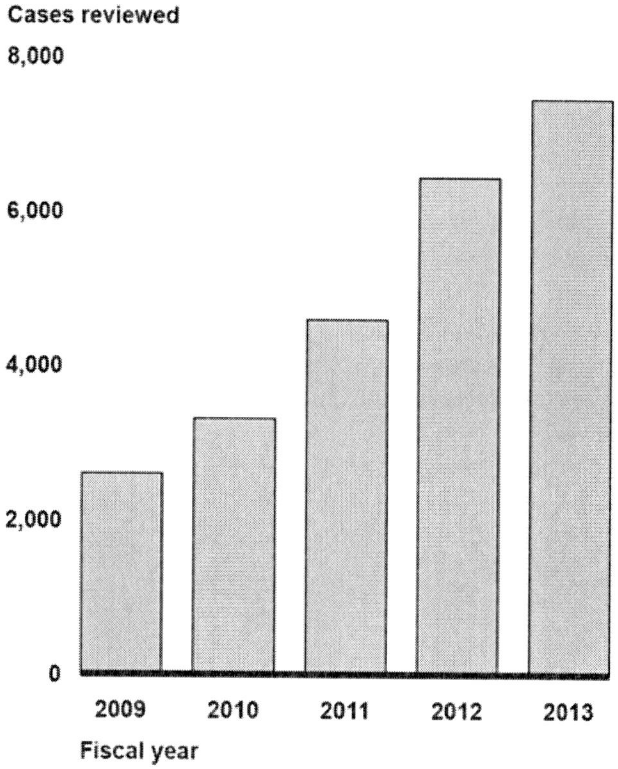

Source: GAO analysis of U.S. Customs and Border Protection data.

Figure 10. Reconsideration Cases Reviewed by the Ombudsman, Fiscal Years 2009-2013.

The Ombudsman told us that the significant increase in the number of reconsideration requests and cumbersome manual processes contribute to delays in completing reconsideration cases. At the time of our visit to the Ombudsman in November 2013, applicants that requested reconsideration of a denial or revocation from a trusted traveler program had to wait about 5 months to learn the outcome of the Ombudsman review. The Ombudsman's office has limited staff who must review every case using manual processes that, according to the Ombudsman, add an additional 1 to 5 days to the review time for each case. For example, at the time of our visit in November 2013, when reviewing a case, the Ombudsman could not document decisions to overturn a denial or revocation directly in the Global Enrollment System (GES)—the trusted travel program's system of record. Instead the Ombudsman sent daily lists of overturned revocations and denials to two different U.S. Customs and Border Protection (CBP) headquarters units for them to unlock these applicants' GES records so that the Ombudsman could later document the outcome of the review and conditionally approve or reinstate the person in GES.

The Department of Homeland Security's (DHS) Office of Inspector General recognized the inefficiencies with the Ombudsman review process and in February 2014 recommended that CBP automate the process and provide adequate staffing to enhance efficiency and effectiveness.[49] CBP concurred with the Inspector General's recommendations and stated that the agency plans to determine the scope and timeline for automating the Ombudsman review process by July 2014. CBP officials told us that they have modified GES to allow the Ombudsman to directly reinstate those who have been revoked within the past year and are considering different options to allow the Ombudsman to document reviews of denials directly in the system. In addition, in March 2014, CBP officials stated they plan to add more staff to address the increase in the requests for reconsideration.

APPENDIX II. PORTS OF ENTRY WITH DEDICATED TRUSTED TRAVELER LANES AND KIOSKS

CBP has dedicated trusted traveler lanes for passenger and commercial traffic at ports of entry along the northern and southern land borders and kiosks for trusted travelers at select international airports in the United States. Table 2 lists ports of entry and specific crossings for the three trusted traveler programs with dedicated lanes at land borders—Secure Electronic Network for Travelers Rapid Inspection (SENTRI), NEXUS, and Free and Secure Trade (FAST).

Table 2. Ports of Entry (POE) and Specific Crossings for Trusted Traveler Programs at Land Borders

Port of entry	Crossings
Secure Electronic Network for Travelers Rapid Inspection (SENTRI)–passenger vehicles and pedestrians along the southern land border	
Brownsville, Texas	• Veterans International
Calexico, California	• Calexico East • Calexico West
Douglas, Arizona	• Douglas
El Paso, Texas	• Stanton Street • Ysleta
Hidalgo, Texas	• Anzalduas • Hidalgo • Pharr
Laredo, Texas	• Lincoln-Juarez
Nogales, Arizona	• Deconcini
Otay Mesa, California	• Otay Mesa
San Luis, Arizona	• San Luis
San Ysidro, California	• San Ysidro
NEXUS–passenger vehicles along the northern land border, and at some Canadian air and seaports for pre-clearance into the United States	
Alexandria Bay, New York	• Thousand Island Bridge
Blaine, Washington	• Pacific Highway • Peace Arch • Point Roberts
Buffalo-Niagara Falls, New York	• Lewiston Bridge • Peace Bridge • Rainbow Bridge • Whirlpool Bridge
Calais, Maine	• International Avenue
Champlain-Rouses Point, New York	• Champlain
Detroit, Michigan	• Ambassador Bridge • Windsor Tunnel
Highgate Springs, Vermont	• Highgate Springs
Houlton, Maine	• Houlton

Table 2. (Continued)

Port of entry	Crossings
Pembina, North Dakota	• Pembina
Port Huron, Michigan	• Blue Water Bridge
Sault Saint Marie, Michigan	• International Bridge
Sumas, Washington	• Sumas
Free and Secure Trade (FAST) South–commercial vehicles along the southern border	
Brownsville, Texas	• Los Tomates • Los Indios
Calexico East, California	• Calexico East
El Paso, Texas	• Bota • Ysleta
Hidalgo, Texas	• Pharr
Laredo, Texas	• Laredo Bridge #4 • Columbia
Nogales, Arizona	• Nogales
Otay Mesa, California	• Otay Mesa
Santa Teresa, New Mexico	• Santa Teresa
FAST North–commercial vehicles along the northern land border	
Blaine, Washington	• Blaine
Champlain-Rouses Point, New York	• Champlain
Detroit, Michigan	• Ambassador Bridge
Port Huron, Michigan	• Blue Water Bridge

Source: GAO analysis of U.S. Customs and Border Protection data.

Table 3 lists airports within the United States with Global Entry kiosks.

Table 3. U.S. Airports with Global Entry Kiosks

Airport
1. Baltimore/Washington International Thurgood Marshall Airport
2. Boston-Logan International Airport
3. Charlotte-Douglas International Airport
4. Chicago O'Hare International Airport
5. Dallas/Ft. Worth International Airport
6. Denver International Airport
7. Detroit Metropolitan Airport

Airport
8. Ft. Lauderdale/Hollywood International Airport
9. George Bush Intercontinental Airport, Houston
10. Hartsfield-Jackson Atlanta International Airport
11. Honolulu International Airport
12. John F. Kennedy International Airport, New York
13. John Wayne Airport, Santa Ana
14. Los Angeles International Airport
15. McCarran International Airport, Las Vegas
16. Miami International Airport
17. Minneapolis/St. Paul International Airport
18. Newark Liberty International Airport
19. Orlando International Airport
20. Orlando-Sanford International Airport
21. Philadelphia International Airport
22. Phoenix Sky Harbor International Airport
23. Portland International Airport,
24. Raleigh-Durham International Airport
25. Salt Lake City International Airport
26. San Antonio International Airport
27. San Diego International Airport
28. San Francisco International Airport
29. Seattle-Tacoma International Airport-SeaTac
30. Tampa International Airport
31. Washington-Dulles International Airport

Source: U.S. Customs and Border Protection data.

APPENDIX III. TRUSTED TRAVELER APPLICATION DENIAL RATES AND REVOCATIONS

The rates at which applicants were denied membership varied by the trusted traveler program and the type of application—whether it was an initial application, a renewal application, or a reapplication.[50] As shown in figure 11, Global Entry and NEXUS had the lowest denial rates for initial applications (4.4 percent and 4.6 percent, respectively) and renewal applications (0.4 percent and 1.0 percent, respectively) from fiscal years 2009 through 2013. For all programs, the denial rates for renewal applications were lowest and the denial rates for reapplications were highest, with the initial application rate being somewhere in between. CBP officials noted that renewal application denial rates are generally low because these applicants have already been approved to participate in a trusted traveler program and have also been subject to ongoing 24-hour vetting. In contrast, CBP officials said that the denial rates for reapplications are higher because these applicants have previously applied for and been denied enrollment in a trusted traveler program and the reason their previous applications were denied may still disqualify them.

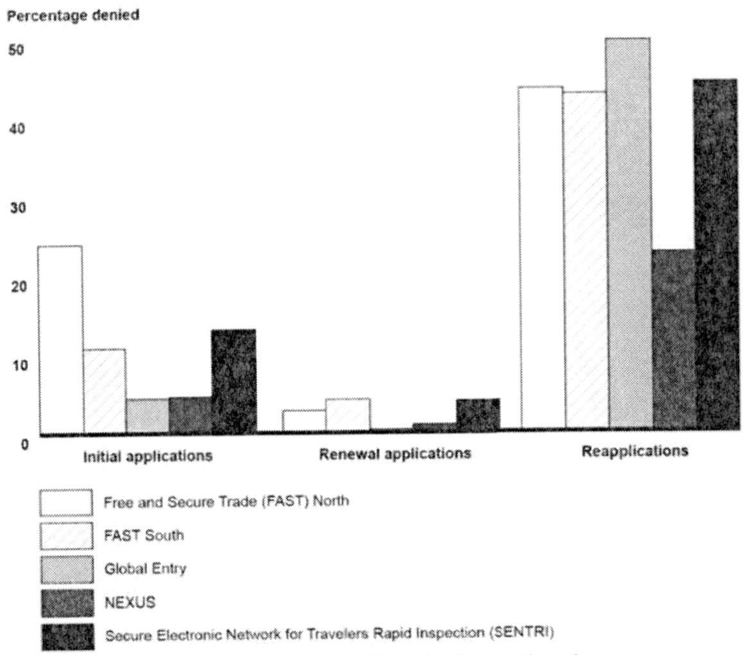

Source: GAO analysis of U.S. Customs and Border Protection data.

Note: Denial rates were calculated by dividing the number of denied applications by the total number of applications adjudicated from fiscal years 2009 through 2013. CBP officials noted that in fiscal year 2009 and part of fiscal year 2010, applications that were abandoned (i.e., the applicant did not schedule an interview or did not show up for his or her scheduled interview) were counted as denials. In fiscal years 2011 through 2013, abandoned applications were not included in the number of denied applications as a result of changes to the Global Enrollment System that allowed CBP to better track abandoned applications.

Figure 11. Trusted Traveler Application Denial Rates for Fiscal Years 2009 through 2013.

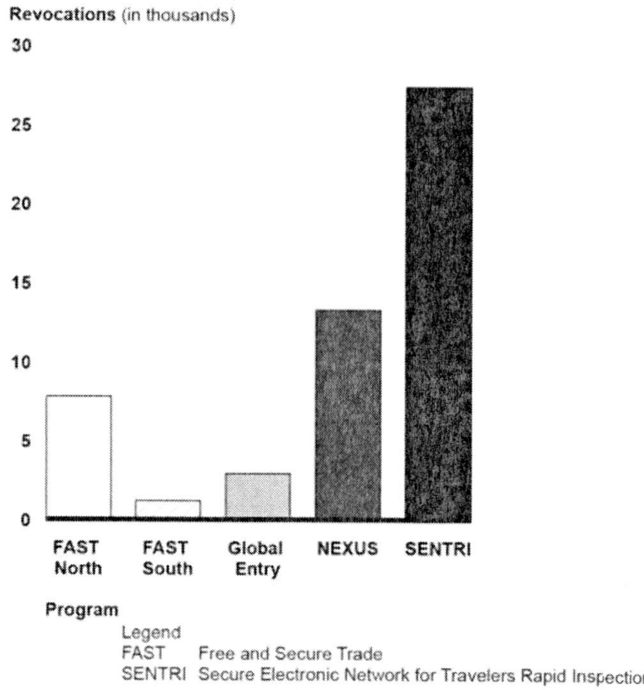

Source: GAO analysis of U.S. Customs and Border Protection data.

Figure 12. Trusted Traveler Revocations as of January 2014.

There have been 52,489 trusted traveler revocations as of January 23, 2014, and the number of revocations varied by program, as shown in figure 12. In particular, there have been more members revoked from SENTRI than from any other program, because, CBP officials explained, the southern border is a higher-risk environment than the northern border. Moreover, CBP officials noted that the number of revocations is relative to the total number of memberships over the lifetime of each program. For example, there are more SENTRI and NEXUS revocations than there are FAST North or FAST South revocations, as SENTRI and NEXUS account for a larger proportion of trusted traveler memberships and have been operating for just as long as or longer than either FAST North or FAST South. Further, while Global Entry accounted for the largest proportion of trusted traveler memberships in January 2014, the number of revocations is relatively low; CBP officials noted it was the most recently implemented trusted traveler program and that the number of revocations has increased as membership has grown.

APPENDIX IV. NUMBER AND PERCENTAGE OF TRUSTED TRAVELER ENTRIES AT PORTS OF ENTRY THAT HAVE TRUSTED TRAVELER LANES, BY PROGRAM, FISCAL YEARS 2009 THROUGH 2013

Tables 4 through 7 show the number of trusted traveler entries at all crossings with dedicated lanes or kiosks, and the percentage of all entries at those crossings that were trusted travelers, by program, for fiscal years 2009 through 2013. The Global Entry table includes only fiscal years 2012 and 2013 because Global Entry was a pilot program until 2012.

Table 4. Number and Percentage of Vehicle Entries through Crossings with Dedicated Secure Electronic Network for Travelers Rapid Inspection (SENTRI) Lanes That Were Trusted Travelers, Fiscal Years 2009 through 2013[a]

Crossing	2009		2010		2011		2012		2013	
	Number	Percent	Number	Percent	Number	Percent	Number	Percent	Number	Percent
Brownsville, TX–Los Tomates (Veterans International)	326,963	27	474,050	33	457,017	35	405,357	31	389,959	32
Calexico, CA–Calexico West Port of Entry	641,121	18	1,139,149	27	1,171,867	29	1,350,604	33	1,467,916	36
Calexico, CA–Calexico East Port of Entry	N/A[b]	N//A	N/A	N/A	236,988	9	434,413	15	496,054	16
Douglas, AZ–Douglas	N/A	N/A	N/A	N/A	N/A	N/A	N/A	N/A	1,995	<1

Crossing	2009		2010		2011		2012		2013	
	Number	Percent	Number	Percent	Number	Percent	Number	Percent	Number	Percent
El Paso, TX–Ysleta	388,937	18	675,955	26	650,589	27	668,660	26	717,120	25
El Paso, TX–Stanton Street	835,536	88	1,196,014	98	1,070,032	95	1,095,821	98	1,098,444	98
Hidalgo, TX–Anzalduas	N/A	N/A	20,315	N/A	40,189	4	N/A	N/A	N/A	N/A
Hidalgo, TX–International Bridge	196,504	6	320,132	10	322,671	12	365,589	15	407,996	18
Hidalgo, TX–Pharr	N/A	N/A	5,302	<1	47,936	4	45,216	4	38,593	3
Laredo, TX–Lincoln Juarez Bridge	587,052	20	1,089,813	31	1,084,706	33	1,076,292	32	1,096,582	31
Nogales, AZ–Nogales	399,281	23	532,775	29	542,358	30	597,625	32	614,254	30
Otay Mesa, CA–Otay Mesa	601,542	17	805,640	20	910,023	22	1,042,229	20	1,256,539	21
San Luis–San Luis	N/A	N/A	N/A	N/A	190,357	9	428,982	18	487,646	18
San Ysidro, CA–San Ysidro	1,951,525	18	3,214,311	24	3,643,708	29	4,079,803	35	4,502,544	40

Source: GAO analysis of U.S. Customs and Border Protection data.

[a] Table entries represent the total number of vehicles entering the United States through dedicated SENTRI lanes, and do not account for SENTRI members entering through regular lanes, or multiple SENTRI members traveling in the same vehicle.

[b] Entries listed as N/A indicate that the listed crossing did not have dedicated SENTRI lanes in that year.

Table 5. Number and Percentage of Vehicle Entries through Crossings with Dedicated NEXUS Lanes That Were Trusted Travelers, Fiscal Years 2009 through 2013[a]

Crossing	2009		2010		2011		2012		2013	
	Number	Percent	Number	Percent	Number	Percent	Number	Percent	Number	Percent
Alexandria Bay, NY–Thousand Island Bridge	N/A[b]	N/A	1,191	<1	1,959	<1	9,849	1	8,635	1
Blaine, WA–Pacific Highway	149,898	15	224,558	17	309,858	20	443,620	25	580,835	32
Blaine, WA–Peace Arch Crossing	370,095	34	380,170	22	464,820	20	861,680	31	1,002,724	34
Buffalo-Niagara Falls, NY–Peace Bridge	281,950	14	350,965	15	377,801	16	402,363	17	415,057	18
Buffalo-Niagara Falls, NY–Queenstown Bridge	2	<1	N/A	N/A	N/A	<1	N/A	<1	6,126	<1
Buffalo- Niagara Falls, NY–Rainbow Bridge	55,183	5	71,329	5	68,051	4	70,399	4	37,559	2.7
Buffalo-Niagara Falls, NY–Whirlpool Bridge	128,429	97	189,396	99	224,479	93	287,670	98	367,190	98
Calais, ME–International Avenue	N/A	N/A	N/A	N/A	N/A	N/A	516	<1	1,625	1
Champlain-Rouses Point–Champlain	19,818	4	39,402	6	45,621	6	54,321	6	60,323	7

Crossing	2009		2010		2011		2012		2013	
	Number	Percent	Number	Percent	Number	Percent	Number	Percent	Number	Percent
Detroit, MI–Ambassador Bridge	275,385	15	397,550	17	387,911	17	439,326	20	444,678	20
Detroit, MI–Windsor Tunnel	158,778	10	244,613	15	248,166	14	271,773	14	299,347	15
Highgate Springs, VT–Highgate Springs	326	<1	1,394	<1	852	<1	2,928	1	3,775	1
Houlton, ME–Houlton	1,088	1	1,593	1	3,253	1	3,632	1	4,729	2
Pembina, ND–Pembina	440	<1	488	<1	217	<1	219	<1	280	0
Point Roberts, WA–Point Roberts	104,950	19	191,296	24	180,609	18	352,088	32	385,363	34
Port Huron, MI–Blue Water Bridge	123,315	10	277,656	17	346,012	19	339,816	18	338,091	17
Sault Saint Marie, MI–International Bridge	980	<1	1,990	<1	2,419	<1	2,982	<1	2,681	<1
Sumas, WA–Sumas	N/A	N/A	N/A	N/A	N/A	N/A	15,172	1	32,069	3

Source: GAO analysis of U.S. Customs and Border Protection data.

[a] Table entries represent the total number of vehicles entering the United States through dedicated NEXUS lanes, and do not account for NEXUS members entering through regular lanes, or multiple NEXUS members traveling in the same vehicle.

[b] Entries listed as N/A indicate that the listed crossing did not have dedicated NEXUS lanes in that year.

Table 6. Number and Percentage of Passenger Entries through Airports for Global Entry Kiosks, Fiscal Years 2012 through 2013

Airport	2012		2013	
	Number	Percent	Number	Percent
Baltimore/Washington International Thurgood Marshall Airport	349	<1	2,642	1
Boston-Logan International Airport	27,371	2	50,579	3
Charlotte-Douglas International Airport	5,183	<1	19,586	2
Chicago O'Hare International Airport	94,287	2	165,720	4
Dallas/Ft. Worth International Airport	66,739	3	116,250	4
Denver International Airport	5,004	1	21,851	4
Detroit Metropolitan Airport	30,527	2	46,915	3
Ft. Lauderdale/Hollywood International Airport	9,997	1	20,334	2
George Bush Intercontinental Airport, Houston	128,270	3	201,163	5
Hartsfield-Jackson Atlanta International Airport	81,494	2	127,063	3
Honolulu International Airport	2,930	<1	6,324	<1
John F. Kennedy International Airport, New York	140,908	1	235,360	2
John Wayne Airport, Santa Ana	189	1	1,224	1
Los Angeles International Airport	78,300	1	135,198	2
McCarran International Airport, Las Vegas	4,547	1	15,432	2
Miami International Airport	116,944	1	206,542	2
Minneapolis/St. Paul International Airport	7,501	1	26,596	3
Newark Liberty International Airport (EWR)	119,448	2	198,283	4
Orlando International Airport	5,718	<1	11,867	1

Airport	2012		2013	
	Number	Percent	Number	Percent
Orlando-Sanford International Airport	51	<1	83	<1
Philadelphia International Airport	15,115	1	32,561	2
Phoenix Sky Harbor International Airport	4,125	1	21,805	3
Portland International Airport	988	1	3,299	2
Raleigh-Durham International Airport	612	1	2,975	5
Salt Lake City International Airport	691	1	3,650	4
San Antonio International Airport	216	<1	5,110	2
San Diego International Airport	1,073	1	6,841	2
San Francisco International Airport	51,127	1	102,521	2
Seattle-Tacoma International Airport-SeaTac	18,560	2	36,530	3
Tampa International Airport	400	<1	3,231	2
Washington-Dulles International Airport	71,216	2	117,544	4

Source: GAO analysis of U.S. Customs and Border Protection data.

Note: Prior to fiscal year 2012, Global Entry was a pilot program. The Global Entry program was expanded to all airports in fiscal year 2012.

Table 7. Number and Percentage of Commercial Vehicle Entries through Ports of Entry with Dedicated Free and Secure Trade (FAST) Lanes That Were Trusted Travelers, Fiscal Years 2009 through 2013

Port of entry	2009		2010		2011		2012		2013	
	Number	Percent	Number	Percent	Number	Percent	Number	Percent	Number	Percent
FAST South										
Brownsville	5,567	3	7,756	4	12,167	6	11,183	5	11,657	6
Calexico	20,098	7	44,170	13	52,192	17	61,507	19	75,443	23
El Paso	51,736	7	11,493	2	152,729	21	159,457	22	159,325	22
Hidalgo	17,393	4	37,895	8	41,264	9	44,142	9	46,114	9
Laredo	34,748	2	79,290	5	142,354	8	160,656	9	181,790	10
Nogales	12,927	5	23,920	7	34,249	12	41,445	14	42,207	14
Otay Mesa	67,573	9	126,138	15	135,377	18	149,094	19	164,553	21
Santa Teresa	357	1	444	1	73	<1	118	<1	290	<1
FAST North										
Blaine	20,518	6	22,261	7	25,781	7	26,294	8	77,931	8
Champlain-Rouses Point	74,223	20	97,466	25	105,817	37	99,205	35	104,082	37
Detroit	230,798	16	288,632	17	280,235	19	307,406	20	307,824	20
Buffalo-Niagara Falls	118,856	12	130,876	13	130,791	14	135,711	14	146,583	16

Source: GAO analysis of U.S. Customs and Border Protection data.

Note: Table entries represent the total number of commercial vehicles entering the United States through dedicated FAST lanes, and do not account for FAST members entering through regular lanes, or multiple FAST members traveling in the same vehicle.

APPENDIX V. CBP EFFORTS TO ADDRESS WAIT TIME DATA LIMITATIONS

CBP faces limitations using vehicle wait time data for public reporting of the wait times themselves and for CBP management decisions across border crossings. In July 2013, we reported on CBP's processes for calculating wait times for commercial vehicles at southwest border land POEs. Specifically, in that report we found that wait times for commercial vehicles along the southern border were unreliable because CBP officers inconsistently implemented one methodology used to calculate wait times, another methodology—driver surveys—was inherently unreliable, and CBP officials used different methodologies to calculate wait times across land border crossings.[51] We recommended that CBP assess the feasibility of replacing current methodologies with automated methods, as well as three other recommendations. CBP concurred with our recommendations. According to CBP officials, CBP uses these same methods to measure wait times for vehicle crossings at all land border POEs for passenger and commercial vehicles, including those with trusted traveler lanes. Therefore, these same limitations apply at all land POEs. In July 2013, we recommended that CBP officials assess the feasibility of replacing current manual wait time calculation methodologies with automated methods.[52] According to CBP officials, reliable passenger wait time data are important at both tactical and strategic levels, and they are working with the private sector to develop different automated wait time technologies. CBP implemented an automated wait time technology using cellular-based technology at the Buffalo-Niagara Falls crossing along the northern border in 2012, and plans to expand the use of the technology. CBP uses the technology by providing select vehicles at the end of the queue with devices that send a wireless signal that are then read by receivers as the cars pass certain checkpoints. In February 2008, the U.S. Department of Transportation Federal Highway Administration initiated pilot projects to develop automated wait time data collection methods at select southwest border crossings that rely on radio- frequency identification readers to read unique signals from passing vehicles at several points along the border-crossing route. As of March 2013, pilot projects to automate wait times were under way or completed at eight locations along the southern border.[53] The results of these pilots could help CBP determine what, if any, method to employ to automate the collection of wait time data. Wait times for Global

Entry are already automated, as each passenger receives a time stamp when his or her flight lands and when clearing primary inspection.

End Notes

[1] Ports of entry are the facilities that provide for the controlled entry into or departure from the United States for persons and materials. Specifically, a port of entry is any officially designated location (seaport, airport, or land border location) where Department of Homeland Security officers or employees are assigned to clear passengers and merchandise, collect duties, and enforce customs laws. A single land port of entry may be composed of one or more crossings. For example, the Port of Laredo, Texas, headed by a port director, oversees operations at four separate border crossings, one rail crossing, and one airport.

[2] The United States has bilateral arrangements with other countries that provide the framework for those countries' participation in Global Entry. The United States also has an arrangement with Canada regarding management of the NEXUS and FAST programs.

[3] See Project Management Institute, *The Standard for Program Management©*, Third Edition, (Newton Square, Pennsylvania: 2013); Office of Management and Budget, *Performance Measurement Challenges and Strategies* (Washington, D.C.: June 2003); and GAO, *Internal Control: Standards for Internal Control in the Federal Government,* GAO/AIMD-00-21.3.1 (Washington, D.C.: November 1999).

[4] SENTRI applicants must pay a $25 application fee when they apply; the total application fee is $122.25, which also includes fees for processing fingerprints and to support the system of dedicated SENTRI lanes. NEXUS and FAST applicants must pay a $50 application fee. Global Entry applicants must pay a $100 application fee.

[5] TECS is designed to be a comprehensive enforcement and communications system that enables CBP and other agencies to create or access lookout data when (1) processing persons and vehicles entering the United States; (2) communicating with other computer systems, such as the Federal Bureau of Investigation's National Crime Information Center; and (3) storing case data and other enforcement reports.

[6] GES is used by CBP to collect and maintain records on individuals who voluntarily provide personally identifiable information for the purpose of enrolling in a trusted traveler program that makes them eligible for expedited processing at designated U.S. POEs.

[7] Trusted traveler applicants can schedule interviews at select enrollment centers; however, some enrollment centers interview applicants only for specific programs. For example, FAST enrollment centers typically do not conduct interviews for the other trusted traveler programs. In addition, SENTRI enrollment centers require a vehicle to be inspected and registered; therefore other trusted traveler enrollment centers cannot finalize the interview process because they do not conduct vehicle inspections. Enrollment centers are generally located at POEs that offer dedicated lanes for trusted travelers.

[8] The trusted traveler Ombudsman reviews cases where an individual has requested reconsideration of a CBP decision after his or her application was denied or membership was revoked.

[9] CBP officials noted that they encountered a higher percentage of FAST applicants with criminal convictions and made the decision to modify the standards for FAST applicants to ensure that multiple misdemeanor convictions do not automatically result in the denial of an application.

[10] C-TPAT is a voluntary program in which CBP officials work with private companies, referred to as partners, to review the security of their international supply chains and improve the security of their shipments to the United States. In return, C-TPAT partners receive various incentives to facilitate the flow of legitimate cargo, such as reduced scrutiny of their

shipments. In October 2006, the Security and Accountability for Every Port Act of 2006 established a statutory framework for the C-TPAT program, codified its existing membership processes, and added new components—such as time frames for certifying, validating, and revalidating members' security practices. 6 U.S.C. §§ 961-973.

[11] Most trusted traveler enrollment centers are located at a POE; however, CBP also has an enrollment center in Washington, D.C., and has also used mobile enrollment centers.

[12] WHTI implements a statutory mandate to require all travelers to present a passport or other document that denotes identity and citizenship when entering the United States. *See* Intelligence Reform and Terrorism Prevention Act of 2004, Pub. L. No. 108-458, § 7209, 118. Stat. 3638, 3823, as amended. The goal of WHTI is to facilitate entry for U.S. citizens and legitimate foreign visitors while strengthening U.S. border security by providing standardized documentation that enables CBP to quickly and reliably identify a traveler. WHTI-approved documents include valid U.S. passports, passport cards, trusted traveler program cards, and others.

[13] Primary inspection booths are where individuals present themselves for inspection to CBP officers for a preliminary screening procedure used to process those individuals who can be readily identified as admissible. Persons whose admissibility cannot be readily determined and persons selected as part of a random selection process are subjected to a more detailed review called a secondary inspection.

[14] Trusted traveler members include both U.S. citizens and citizens from other countries. See figure 4 for additional information on the citizenship of trusted travelers.

[15] We are currently reviewing TSA's Pre-Check program and plan to issue a report on the subject later this year.

[16] The number of crossings for SENTRI, NEXUS, and FAST indicates the number of vehicles entering through those programs, regardless of the number of passengers in each vehicle, and does not include pedestrian entries. The number of crossings for Global Entry includes the number of individual people entering the United States through the program. For all four programs, individual travelers and vehicles are counted each time they entered the country, and therefore an individual traveler or vehicle could account for more than one crossing.

[17] Prior to fiscal year 2012, Global Entry was a pilot program.

[18] One crossing along the southern border had only SENTRI lanes.

[19] One crossing along the northern border had only NEXUS lanes.

[20] Fiscal year 2013 data are from October 2012 through June 2013.

[21] Office of Management and Budget, *Performance Measurement Challenges and Strategies* (Washington, D.C.: June 2003).

[22] GAO/AIMD-00-21.3.1.

[23] The number of applications includes first-time applications, renewal applications, and "reapplications"—applications from applicants who have applied for the program one or more times previously. In addition to its responsibility to vet these types of applications, the Vetting Center conducts ongoing vetting of current members and may also have to revet members when they update their personal information.

[24] CBP officials noted that applicants who have been conditionally approved by the Vetting Center but have not yet completed the enrollment interview are subject to 24-hour vetting.

[25] CBP officials stated that they observed many interviews and came to the conclusion that the interview process could be completed in a 15-minute time frame.

[26] In February 2014, the DHS Office of the Inspector General recommended that CBP pursue eliminating the vehicle inspection during the initial SENTRI enrollment interview. See DHS Office of Inspector General, *Ensuring the Integrity of CBP's Secure Electronic Network for Travelers Rapid Inspection Program*, OIG-14-32 (Washington, D.C.: February 2014). In March 2014, CBP officials told us they were considering options to revise the SENTRI vehicle examination requirement in response to this recommendation.

[27] Project Management Institute, *The Standard for Program Management©*, Third Edition.

[28] The daily report from March 19, 2013, lists 68 enrollment centers, but the data indicate that 3 of the enrollment centers were not scheduling interviews, so we omitted these from the total number of enrollment centers. Additional enrollment centers opened over the time period we reviewed for this report—fiscal year 2009 through January 2014—so the total number of enrollment centers will vary by date.

[29] The daily report from January 23, 2014, lists 83 enrollment centers, but the data indicate that 4 of the enrollment centers were not scheduling interviews, so we omitted these from the total number of enrollment centers. Additional enrollment centers opened over the time period we reviewed for this report—fiscal year 2009 through January 2014—so the total number of enrollment centers will vary by date.

[30] GAO/AIMD-00-21.3.1.

[31] CBP's Self Inspection Program covers operational requirements other than those of the trusted traveler programs.

[32] A CBP daily report from January 23, 2014, lists a total of 83 enrollment centers, but the data indicate that 4 of the enrollment centers were not scheduling interviews.

[33] The other 9 enrollment centers we visited did not have locally developed trusted traveler interview question lists.

[34] We analyzed the denial rates at those enrollment centers that adjudicated 100 initial applications or more for a particular program in that fiscal year to facilitate comparison, since percentages for data from relatively small populations can change greatly with minor changes in the data. Our analysis covers fiscal years 2011 through 2013 because CBP officials noted that in fiscal year 2009 and part of fiscal year 2010, applications that were abandoned (i.e., the applicant did not schedule an interview or did not show up for the scheduled interview) were counted as denials.

[35] A statistical analysis we conducted found that these differences were significant, that is, there was less than a 0.001 percent chance that each of these differences was equal to zero. Specifically, we estimated t-statistics for the difference between each pair of denial rates, assuming unequal variances, and then calculated the associated two-tailed p-value. We limited our statistical analysis to the largest denial rate range for each program among enrollment centers with at least 100 applications.

[36] CBP officials noted that most applicants are U.S. citizens and thus there would not be any admissibility concerns for these applicants.

[37] GAO/AIMD-00-21.3.1.

[38] The nine countries with operational joint trusted traveler programs with the United States as of March 2014 are Canada, Germany, Mexico, the Netherlands, Panama, Qatar, the Republic of Korea, Saudi Arabia, and the United Kingdom. DHS has signed joint statements with Australia, Israel, and New Zealand to explore implementing joint trusted traveler programs in the future. The bilateral arrangements are nonbinding and may be discontinued by either country, according to CBP.

[39] Canadian citizens may enroll in NEXUS and use the Global Entry kiosks when entering the United States through aviation POEs.

[40] GAO/AIMD-00-21.3.1.

[41] CBP weights its calculations for average wait times at land borders using vehicle volumes in order to account for differences in traffic flow at different times of day and on different days, according to CBP officials.

[42] We have previously reported that CBP wait time data are unreliable because CBP officers inconsistently implemented an approved data collection methodology, and the methodologies used vary by crossing. GAO, *U.S.-Mexico Border: CBP Action Needed to Improve Wait Time Data and Measure Outcomes of Trade Facilitation Efforts*, GAO-13-603 (Washington, D.C.: July 24, 2013). For this reason, we determined that we could not reliably compare specific wait times across crossings. At each individual crossing, however, CBP uses the same methodology to estimate average wait times for trusted and regular travelers. We are therefore reporting estimated differences in the average wait times for

trusted and regular travelers at individual crossings. For more information about the reliability of CBP's wait time data, see appendix V.

[43] At one of the other 3 crossings with SENTRI lanes, regular travelers waited less than 15 minutes longer than trusted travelers on average. Another converted its SENTRI lanes to regular lanes in fiscal year 2012, and the third had only SENTRI lanes in fiscal year 2013.

[44] Pedestrian crossers of the northern and southern land borders are eligible for NEXUS and SENTRI, but as the majority of users of these programs are drivers and vehicle passengers, we are limiting this analysis to vehicle traffic across the borders.

[45] The differences in wait times are based on the reported average wait times for all regular travelers and for trusted travelers from the point at which they are able to enter dedicated lanes. According to CBP officials, at some POEs, particularly along the northern border, infrastructure constraints such as bridges cause trusted travelers to wait with regular travelers until they are able to reach dedicated lanes.

[46] At 2 of the other northern border crossings with NEXUS lanes, regular travelers waited an estimated 16 minutes longer than regular travelers on average. The third had only NEXUS lanes.

[47] One of the other crossings with a SENTRI lane converted its SENTRI lane to a regular lane in fiscal year 2012 and therefore did not have SENTRI inspections in fiscal year 2013. For the other, which first opened its trusted traveler lanes in 2013, the average inspection time was 47 seconds. Inspection times at the other 6 crossings with NEXUS lanes ranged from 31 seconds to 66 seconds on average in fiscal year 2013.

[48] CBP defines inspection time as the time a traveler spends with a CBP officer. Because Global Entry primary screening is conducted through kiosks, CBP does not calculate an average inspection time for Global Entry primary screenings. At the 3 other crossings with SENTRI lanes, 2 had either only trusted or only regular traveler lanes, and at the other, the average inspection time was nearly the same for trusted and regular travelers. At the other 7 crossings with NEXUS lanes, 5 had slightly longer average inspection times for regular travelers, which ranged from 9 to 16 seconds longer than the average inspection times for trusted travelers, 1 had a longer inspection time for trusted travelers, and the last had only NEXUS lanes and therefore did not report inspection times for regular traffic.

[49] DHS Office of Inspector General, *Ensuring the Integrity of CBP's Secure Electronic Network for Travelers Rapid Inspection Program*, OIG-14-32 (Washington, D.C.: February 2014).

[50] A reapplication is the application of someone who has applied for a trusted traveler program one or more times previously and has been denied.

[51] GAO-13-603.

[52] GAO-13-603.

[53] The completed pilot project was at Otay Mesa (Otay Mesa, California,) and the ongoing projects were at Pharr (Pharr, Texas), Bridge of the Americas (El Paso, Texas), Ysleta (El Paso, Texas), World Trade Bridge (Laredo, Texas), Columbia Solidarity Bridge (Laredo, Texas), Veterans (Brownsville, Texas), and Mariposa (Nogales, Arizona).

In: Trusted Traveler Programs
Editor: Blaire Forester
ISBN: 978-1-63321-830-7

Chapter 2

STATEMENT OF COLLEEN MANAHER, EXECUTIVE DIRECTOR, PLANNING, PROGRAM ANALYSIS, AND EVALUATION, U.S. CUSTOMS AND BORDER PROTECTION. HEARING ON "FEDERAL GOVERNMENT APPROACHES TO ISSUING BIOMETRIC IDS: PART II"*

INTRODUCTION

Chairman Mica, Ranking Member Connolly, Members of the Subcommittee, it is a privilege and an honor to appear before you to discuss the work of U.S. Customs and Border Protection (CBP), particularly with regard to CBP's development of the minimum standards and best practices for the issuance of cross border travel documents through the Western Hemisphere Travel Initiative (WHTI), CBP's Trusted Traveler Programs and the use of biometrics to secure these programs.

As America's frontline border agency, CBP's priority mission is to protect the American public, while facilitating lawful travel and trade. To do this, CBP has deployed a multi-layered, risk-based approach to enhance the

* This is an edited, reformatted and augmented version of a statement presented June 19, 2013 before the House Committee on Oversight and Government Reform, Subcommittee on Government Operations.

security of the people and goods entering the United States. This layered approach to security reduces our reliance on any single point or program that could be compromised.

On a typical day, CBP welcomes nearly a million travelers at our air, land, and sea ports. The volume of international air travelers increased by 12 percent from 2009 to 2012 and is projected to increase 4 to 5 percent each year for the next five years[1]. CBP continues to address the security elements of its mission while meeting the challenge of increasing volumes of travel in air, land, and sea environments, by assessing the risk of passengers from the earliest, and furthest, possible point, and at each point in the travel continuum.

Working with our partners, CBP secures our Nation's borders by employing and enhancing our layers of defense throughout the entire supply chain (for goods) and transit sequence (for people) – starting from their points of origin, transit to the United States, to their arrival and entry at our ports of entry. These layers rely upon increased intelligence and risk-management strategies regarding the movement and flow of both travelers and trade. Risk segmentation, separating the "knowns" from the "unknowns" allows us to enhance security by focusing more attention on stopping illegitimate trade, while at the same time facilitating legitimate travel and commerce.

More than 1.9 million people, including more than 425,000 new members this fiscal year, have enrolled in Trusted Traveler Programs, which allow expedited clearance for pre-approved, low-risk travelers upon arrival in the United States. These trusted travelers carry credentials that meet or exceed the International Organization for Standardization security standards and exceed the best practices for protection of personal identification documents.

Western Hemisphere Travel Initiative (WHTI)

In 2009, CBP implemented a key 9/11 Commission recommendation through WHTI and established the minimum requirements for cross-border travel documents with the states, tribes and Canada. This program involved a substantial technology investment in the land border environment that continues to provide both facilitation and security benefits. Today, as a result of WHTI, more than 20 million Radio Frequency Identification (RFID) technology-enabled travel documents have been issued. These documents are more secure, as they can be verified electronically in real-time back to the issuing authority to establish identity and citizenship; they also reduce the average vehicle processing time by 20 percent.

A direct result of the increased use of RFID-enabled secure travel documents is CBP's capability to increase the national law enforcement query rate, including queries against the terrorist watch list, to more than 98 percent. By comparison, in 2005, CBP performed law enforcement queries in the land border environment for only 5 percent of travelers.

OVERVIEW OF TRUSTED TRAVELER PROGRAMS

CBP operates four international trusted traveler programs offering expedited processing for pre-identified, lower risk populations. These programs improve security by increasing efficiencies in allocating screening resources, and facilitate legitimate trade and travel. Membership in these programs is valid for five years, and the application process, membership requirements, and standard of vetting are the same.

Applicants who voluntary participate in the program undergo the following: a biographical background check against criminal, law enforcement, customs, immigration, and terrorist indices; a 10-fingerprint law enforcement check; and a personal interview with a CBP officer.

Fingerprints are checked against the FBI database for criminal history and also are run against and stored in the DHS Automated Biometric Identity System, IDENT, which is used to perform the biometric match during the primary inspection. CBP also conducts recurrent vetting checks every 24-hours. As a result of the recurring vetting, if an individual is found to no longer be eligible to participate in the program the individual's membership will be immediately revoked and subsequently they will be notified of the revocation.

Once enrolled, applicants are issued a RFID-enabled card that identifies their record and status in CBP's database upon arrival at a port. There are many security features on the Trusted Traveler cards. The personal data on the cards are laser engraved. The documents use a combination of printed and electronic security features. Some of the printed features can be seen, others cannot. An antenna and RFID chip embedded within the card help to verify the identity of the bearer to Customs and Border Protection Officers while optical security features help officers quickly validate that both the traveler and card are authentic.

Secure Electronic Network for Travelers Rapid Inspection (SENTRI)

The Secure Electronic Network for Travelers Rapid Inspection, also referred to as the SENTRI program, offers pre-approved, low-risk travelers expedited entry into the U.S. through designated lanes at the U.S.-Mexico land border ports. In addition to the standard vetting process, and an RFID enabled card, the SENTRI program requires a vehicle or motorcycle inspection to take place. A sticker decal is issued once complete. SENTRI users have access to specific, dedicated primary lanes into the U.S.

SENTRI was first implemented at Otay Mesa, CA, in 1995, and has grown to include the ten largest southern border POEs along the U.S.-Mexico border. SENTRI members currently account for 19 percent of all cross SWB traffic. The fee for SENTRI is $122.25.

NEXUS

NEXUS is a bilateral program with the Canada Border Services Agency (CBSA), which offers pre-approved, low-risk travelers expedited travel between the U.S. and Canada through designated lanes and kiosks at the land border and all Canadian preclearance airports, as well as in the marine environment for pleasure boaters. NEXUS identifies low-risk travelers through: a complete biographic check; an interview with a CBP officer and a CBSA officer; and a biometric (fingerprint) criminal history check.

Once identified as low-risk, applicants are enrolled in NEXUS and given a RFID-enabled card that is unique to the traveler. The card allows the traveler to use dedicated primary lanes at land border POEs reserved for NEXUS member use. At the Canadian airports that have NEXUS Air kiosks, passengers use kiosks instead of dedicated lanes; and iris scans identify low-risk travelers. NEXUS Air kiosks uses a biometric identifier (iris) in place of RFID-enabled cards like at the land border dedicated lanes. At the time of enrollment, travelers qualify for trusted traveler status in all modes of travel (air, sea and land).

In FY 2012, the average NEXUS program lane processing time, 20 seconds, was two and a half times faster than vehicles processed at general lanes crossing the northern border (general lane times along the northern border average 50 seconds per vehicle). For FY 2012, the NEXUS program lanes produced an inspection time savings equivalent to 24 CBP officers. The fee for NEXUS is $50.

Free and Secure Trade (FAST)

CBP's Free and Secure Trade, more commonly known as FAST is the cargo equivalent of the SENTRI and NEXUS facilitative programs. Through FAST, importers, commercial carriers, truck drivers and manufacturers who enroll in the program and meet agreed upon security criteria, including participation in the C-TPAT program, are granted expedited clearance at a POE. Using electronic data transmission and transponder technology, CBP expedites clearance of approved trade participants. FAST supports a more secure supply chain and enables CBP to focus security efforts and inspections on high-risk commerce, where the attention is most needed. The fee for FAST is $50.

Global Entry (GE)

GE, CBP's newest trusted traveler program, which launched in 2008, is aimed at facilitating low-risk travelers in the air environment. CBP designed GE for expedited clearance of pre-approved low-risk air travelers into the U.S. using automated kiosks, placed in the Federal Inspection Services area of each identified airport, allowing GE enrolled travelers to bypass queues and process through Passport Control without having to see a CBP officer. GE facilitated entry into the U.S. is especially beneficial to frequent international flyers. Currently, GE is available at Atlanta, Baltimore, Boston, Charlotte, Chicago, Dallas/Ft. Worth, Denver, Detroit, Ft. Lauderdale, Guam, Honolulu, Houston, John Wayne Orange County, Las Vegas, Los Angeles, Miami, Minneapolis, Newark, New York (JFK), Orlando, Philadelphia, Phoenix, Portland (OR), Raleigh-Durham, San Antonio, Salt Lake City, Sanford (FL), San Juan, San Diego, San Francisco, Saipan, Seattle, Tampa, and Washington Dulles airports. GE is also available at all eight Canadian preclearance sites - Calgary, Edmonton, Halifax, Montreal, Ottawa, Toronto, Vancouver, and Winnipeg; at two preclearance sites in Ireland - Dublin and Shannon; and two U.S. territory sites - Guam and Saipan.

GE membership is currently available to U.S. citizens, U.S. lawful permanent residents (LPRs), and Mexican nationals. Canadian citizens and residents may enjoy GE benefits through membership in the NEXUS program. Additionally, in a joint arrangement with the Netherlands, CBP allows Dutch citizens to participate in GE, and U.S. citizens to participate in the Dutch trusted traveler program, Privium. A joint arrangement with South Korea allows Korean citizens to participate in GE, and U.S. citizens to participate in the South Korean Trusted Traveler program, the Smart Entry System. CBP is operating pilot programs with Germany, Qatar, and the United Kingdom, allowing limited numbers of their citizens to participate in Global Entry. Once CBP enters into a bilateral agreement, a pilot may be conducted at the request of the partner country to test the application and vetting systems of the partner country before the program is formally launched. GE members use automated kiosks located in the Federal Inspection Services (FIS) area of each program airport. Kiosk transactions are initiated by inserting the member's travel document (passport or lawful permanent resident card) into the document reader. Through fingerprint biometrics and passport or LPR card data, the GE kiosk: validates membership eligibility; performs real time law enforcement database queries; and allows the traveler to complete CBP Declarations questions via touch screen. Upon successful completion of the GE process at the kiosk, the traveler will be issued a transaction receipt and directed to baggage claim and the exit, unless chosen for a selective or random secondary referral. Global Entry Members are also issued a card, however this is not for use of the kiosk. These cards may be used at the land borders. The cards allow GE members to make use of the NEXUS and SENTRI lanes when travelling into the U.S. via the land borders.

To date, more than 718,000 travelers have enrolled in the Global Entry program. Global Entry has reduced average wait times for Global Entry users by more than 70 percent for the participants, with more than 75 percent of travelers using Global Entry processed in less than five minutes. The 283 Global Entry kiosks have been used nearly 5 million times, equal to approximately 83,300 CBP inspectional processing hours. These hours are then expended on the normal passenger processing, helping to reduce overall wait times. The fee for Global entry is $100.

Costs vs Cost Savings

CBP is conducting a new fee study, expected to be complete by the end of this year, for its Trusted Traveler Programs. Once the fee study is complete, DHS will publish a Federal Register Notice, which will include a comment period. To support Trusted Traveler Programs, CBP is authorized to use approximately $6 million in appropriated funding each fiscal year. Appropriated funds are complemented with over $30M in revenues (user fee collections fluctuate due to economic factors and cycles of enrollment renewals) generated by enrollment fees. Combined resources are used to fund staff vetting applications, and equipment and maintain information systems. In addition, the cost avoidance of these programs in terms of inspectional hours saved due to the increased efficiencies and faster processing times is the equivalent of $21.6 million, or 220,860 inspectional hours saved.

Conclusion

To counter the threat of terrorism and secure our borders, while expeditiously facilitating legitimate trade and travel, CBP relies on a balanced mix of professional law enforcement personnel, advanced technologies and modernized facilities and infrastructure both at and between the ports of entry. With the support of Congress, CBP has made significant progress in securing the borders through a multi-layered approach using a variety of tools at our disposal. CBP will continue to work within DHS and with our federal, state, local, tribal, and international partners, to strengthen border security. We must remain vigilant and focus on building our approach to position CBP's greatest capabilities to combat the greatest risks that exist today, to be prepared for emerging threats, and to continue to build a sophisticated approach tailored to meet the challenges of securing a 21st century border.

We are continuing to enhance and expand our trusted traveler programs, which expedite the processing of known, low-risk travelers so that we can better focus our attention on higher-risk, unknown travelers.

Chairman Mica, Ranking Member Connolly, Members of the Subcommittee, thank you for this opportunity to testify about the work of CBP and our efforts in securing our borders. We look forward to answering your questions.

End Note

[1] U.S. Commerce Department Forecast of Growth in International Travel to the United States Through 2016. http://www.commerce.gov/news/press-releases/2012/04/23/us-commerce-department-forecasts-growth-international-travel-united-s.

INDEX